Shortcuts To

Bliss

The 50 Best Ways to Improve Relationships,
Connect with Spirit, and Make Your Dreams Come True

Jonathan Robinson

CONARI PRESS
Berkeley, California

Conari Press books are distributed by Publishers Group West.

ISBN: 1-57324-137-7

Cover Design: Ame Beanland
Cover Illustration: Kurt Vargo
Interior Illustrations: Ashleigh Brilliant

Library of Congress Cataloging-in-Publication Data
Robinson, Jonathan
Shortcuts to bliss : the 50 best ways to improve relationships,
connect with spirit, and make your dreams come true / Jonathan Robinson.
p.   cm.
ISBN: 1-57324-137-7 (pbk.)
1. Self-help techniques.   I. Title
BF632.R64   1998

158—dc21   98-24238
                                                        CIP

Printed in the United States of America on recycled paper.
1   3   5   7   9   10   8   6   4   2

Contents

section four

Connecting with Spirit

section five

Living Your Dreams

Introduction

The dictionary defines "bliss" as "great happiness or joy." It's what we all ultimately want. Unfortunately, in our fast paced world of endless distractions, it can be hard to come by. If you're like me, you want to feel great, but you don't like having to read hundreds of pages in self-help books in order to find just a couple of useful ideas. That's why I wrote this book. In this book, you'll get almost no theory or "filler" information—just remarkable "shortcuts" to the life you desire. You'll learn about fifty incredibly powerful and practical tools for personal and spiritual fulfillment. These methods will help you have better relationships, increased success and enjoyment in your career, a more loving connection with your self, and a lot more fun in your life.

In my psychotherapy practice and in seminars I lead across the country, I've carefully noted exactly which ideas and techniques people have found to be the most helpful. I often refer to them as "power tools" because of their almost magical effect on people's lives. Think of the difference in power between an electric saw and a hand saw and you'll have an idea of how effective these tools and ideas can be. In this day and age of high stress and little time, we need all the help we can get to make positive changes in our lives. When people are unaware of these methods for transformation, they often end up staying stuck, or spending a lot of needless energy using techniques that are ineffective.

Recently, a client came to see me for psychotherapy complaining of depression. She hated her job, was overweight, and her marriage was "just about over." I taught her three simple methods that I outline in this book. In a short period of time her whole life had turned around. When she called me after a couple of months, she stated, "I feel like a whole new woman who just stepped into a brand new life. I quit my job and found one I really enjoy, my marriage is better than ever, and I've lost over twenty pounds. Those methods you taught me really work. I'm amazed!" Some methods are simply very effective. If a person was unaware that airplanes exist, it would seem miraculous to go from New York to London in a single day. Yet, to anyone who knew about planes, it would seem simple. In the same way, once you know about these tools, you'll create seemingly miraculous results in your life with little effort.

This book has methods and ideas for various aspects of life, from finding an intimate partner to finding the peace within. *You need not read this book from start to finish.* Instead, feel free to look in the Table of Contents for a heading that sounds like something you'd really like to know about. Then, turn to that section to explore what magical method awaits your discovery. The only way to know how effective the techniques in this book really are is by trying them out. Often, simply reading about a method gives no clue as to what the actual experience is like. For example, if you knew nothing about making love, but you read a scientific description of how to "do it," it would not seem like a very special way to spend your time. In a similar way, some of these techniques may sound strange, but they can create miracles in your life. If you try them with an open mind and heart, I know you'll be pleased with the results you receive.

As we get ready to enter the third millennium, we are being presented with technological changes that are mind numbing in complexity and scope. In order to thrive in this "new world," we need to be able to quickly make internal shifts that allow us to handle the new stresses we face. The methods presented in this book are some of the best, easiest, most effective and practical "inner technology" you'll find for creating the life you really want. The ultimate computer is right between your ears. The fifty tools in this book will give you the edge you need to create a life of success, love, peace, and joy. In a word—bliss. Enjoy.

NO MATTER
WHAT YOU
MAY THINK,
I DO NOT
ENJOY SUFFERING.

AT LEAST,
NOT VERY MUCH.

Feeling Really Good

$\mathscr{A}$ single psychological principle unites all people who have ever lived: Every human being wants to avoid emotional or physical pain and gain emotional or physical pleasure. Of course, how we accomplish this task is different for each of us. To feel good, some people have to control and manipulate millions of people, while others need only close their eyes and meditate. If the ways you know of feeling great take a lot of time or money or involve a lot of effort, you reduce the odds of feeling happy much of the time. On the other hand, if you know a variety of simple ways of feeling loving, peaceful and joyous, you'll probably experience a lot more pleasure in your life. Likewise, if your methods for avoiding pain are harmful to you (such as drug use, overeating, etc.), your quality of life will go down. Yet if you know healthy and effective ways to overcome pain, then suffering need not be your constant companion.

Each culture has prescribed ways of avoiding pain and gaining pleasure. For example, in Western culture we're conditioned to believe that if we only had more money, we'd definitely be happier. Surprisingly, studies show that once a person achieves middle-class status, additional money has no effect on their level of fulfillment. Yet many people struggle for years to make it rich, only to find that they aren't any happier. By the time most people have realized that what they *thought* would make them satisfied hasn't really worked, it's too late for them to explore other avenues.

If money isn't the key to happiness and pleasure, what is? In general, research indicates that people who feel connected to a spiritual purpose, are achieving meaningful goals, and have satisfying relationships are the happiest. In other sections in this book, I talk about ways to move forward in each of these areas of life. In this section, I describe simple ways to *directly* bring more pleasure and less pain into your life. I have found that when a person feels good most of the time, it's easier to pursue satisfying relationships and meaningful goals.

Unlike most ways we've been taught to feel better, the methods in this section can generally be done in under two minutes, they don't cost anything, and they're immediately effective. In addition, many popular ways to change how we feel have negative side effects, whereas these methods tend to actually be good for you. By learning simple ways to change how you feel, you'll have a lot more energy for pursuing what's really important to you. Having a sense of control over one's emotions can give a person greater "riches" than material wealth. As you practice these methods, you'll begin to feel more in charge of your feelings, your life, and ultimately, your destiny.

1. How to Quickly Change How You Feel

The Art of Asking the Right Questions

aving written two books that consist mostly of questions (*The Little Book Of Big Questions* and *Instant Insight*), I have a lot I could say about this subject. Yet, in essence what I want to convey is that by asking yourself specific questions on a regular basis, you can dramatically change your life. Questions are a quick and powerful way to change your focus—and what you focus on grows. Our emotional state is largely determined by what we think about. If we subconsciously think throughout the day, "What else is wrong in my life?" then we'll likely feel anxious a lot of the time. However, if we focus on the question, "What can I feel grateful for?" then it's easy to feel a whole lot better.

Asking questions to change your focus is a time-tested technique. We already do it, and it has an immense impact on how we feel. Unfortunately, usually we use this method to make ourselves feel angry, depressed, or anxious. We think of things like, "What else do I have to do today?" or "Why is that person such a jerk?" Like a good computer, our brain attempts to answer whatever question we feed it. Out of the millions of things it could think about, our mind chooses just a few things to focus on. How does it know what to let into consciousness, and what to ignore? Our brain chooses what to perceive based on the subconscious (or conscious) questions we ask ourselves. If you ask a negative question, you'll likely feel morose. If you ask a positive one, you'll focus on different thoughts and likely end up feeling good.

Over many years of trial and error, I have found there are four specific questions that are effective in quickly changing how a person feels. They are:

1) What small successes have I had recently?

2) What could I feel grateful for?

3) Who do I love and/or who loves me?

4) What do I appreciate about myself?

Each of these questions can be like a flashlight that helps you see past your inner darkness to the "heaven within." It only takes one or two minutes of focusing on any of these inquiries to change what you perceive and how you feel. To tune into the magic they offer, simply begin by taking a slow, deep breath, and then repeat the chosen question a couple of times. At first you'll probably come up with intellectual answers that don't seem very connected to your feelings. Yet with practice you'll learn to feel positive emotions that result from the answers you think of; for example, if you find yourself feeling overwhelmed, you may choose to ask yourself, "What small successes have I had recently?" As you think of several answers, you'll notice your thoughts will begin to move in a different direction. By focusing and visualizing one or more successes, you can begin to tune into the *feelings* of confidence and achievement. In just a couple of minutes you can transform your experience and feel immensely better.

When you answer any of the four inquiries, the important thing is to think of *specific* instances when you felt what the question is asking you about. They need not be big, dramatic examples—they only need to be times that were emotionally meaningful to you. For instance, when asking yourself, "What could I feel grateful for?" you could feel thankful for literally hundreds of things. You could feel gratitude for being healthy, for having food when much of the world goes hungry, for friends, or even for the use of your telephone. By focusing on how fortunate you are compared to many other people, you can learn to tune into the feeling of gratitude whenever you desire.

The question "Who do I love and who loves me?" can be a wonderful way to dive into your heart and experience the grace of love. By remembering a specific time you felt loved by someone, or a particular time you felt in love with someone, it's possible to tune into the warmth within your heart. With practice, you can take "mini love breaks" throughout the day that open your heart with love in just a minute of meditation.

The final question "What do I appreciate about myself?" can be a good antidote to feelings of self-dislike or unworthiness. The simple fact that you bought this book shows that you're interested in bettering yourself. You probably have a lot of little things about yourself which are likeable. By thinking of some of them, you'll feel better. For some people it's hard to see what is good and loveable about themselves. If you have a hard time with this question, you might try asking yourself, "What good things would my friends say about me?" As you focus on what you (or others) see as your positive traits, you'll feel more confident, loveable, and have genuine compassion for yourself.

The hardest thing about this technique is remembering to use it. Yet if you give it a really good try, you'll see that it can work wonders. Being able to quickly go from feeling overwhelmed to feeling confident, or feeling anxious to being grateful is one of the most important skills a person could learn. To a large extent, your ability to act effectively in the world is based on how good you feel. As you gain more control over your thoughts and emotions by asking yourself these four questions, you'll not only feel better—but you'll also be better able to contribute to others.

2. How to Easily Become a Happier Person

The Pain and Pleasure List

What do you absolutely love to do? It need not be a big thing. Perhaps you really love to watch football, or maybe you really enjoy baking your own bread. Often, we get so caught up in living our life that we forget to take time for life's simple pleasures. Many people find that their life is so full of responsibilities that they rarely take time for fun and adventure. If that sounds like you, then you'll benefit by using the "Pain and Pleasure List" (PPL). The PPL is a list of at least ten things you enjoy doing and a list of ten things you don't particularly care for. It helps you clarify what really turns you on in life and what you do only because you have to—or think you should. While we all need to do things we don't like from time to time, life is not meant to be a series of burdens and responsibilities. By having this handy list that says so much about yourself, you'll be able to make important changes in your life with a lot more ease.

The first step in using the PPL is to simply create the list. The singular act of writing down ten things you love to do and ten you don't care for can reveal a lot about your life. Recently, a client named James made his list while in my office. He had originally come to see me because of depression, stress at work, and problems with his wife. This was the list he created:

Ten Things I *Don't* Like to Do.

1. Go to work.
2. Market myself or my products.
3. Clean the house.
4. Cook.
5. Be around disagreeable people.
6. Spend time with my parents.
7. Taxes and paying the bills.
8. Give my wife a massage.
9. Go shopping for clothes or gifts.
10. Argue with wife.

Ten Things I *Love* to Do

Ride my bike.

Be by myself, reading a good book.

Play with the dog.

Eat good food.

Travel.

Get a massage.

Spend time in nature.

Make love with my wife.

Drive and listen to music.

Watch a good football game.

After James made his list, I had him estimate the number of hours every month he spent doing each activity. When he finished this part of the exercise, it was brutally clear why he was depressed, stressed, and messed-up with his wife. The total number of hours on the "pain" side of the list was a whopping 215 hours per month. The total number of hours on the "pleasure" side of the list was a meager 32 hours a month. That's almost a seven-to-one ratio of pain to pleasure. I've found that when the degree of pain as compared to pleasure rises above a five-to-one ratio, people dislike their life. In order to feel good again, such people need to spend less time doing "painful" activities, and more time doing what they enjoy.

The first key to changing your life and behavior is to be *aware* of what's currently not working. If, after completing your own PPL, you see a similar pattern to James' then you'll know you've been denying yourself too much. You need to put pleasurable activities at a greater level of importance in your life. Sometimes people think if they make pleasure a bigger priority, the rest of their life will fall apart. Not true. When we *don't* have enough good times in our life, we become less capable and effective in our career and relationships. We pay a price. As we feel good more regularly, the " rising sea" of our emotions tends to lift the various "boats" of our life.

On the other hand, some people who complete the PPL see a pattern of having *too much* pleasure in their life. They tend to avoid responsibilities and discipline at all costs. Unfortunately, this form of hedonism doesn't work well long term. By avoiding difficult things now, people with this predilection often create problems in their finances and relationships later on. The key to having a successful life is to find the right balance of pain to pleasure. It must be a balance that works, not only in one's current life, but it must also work long term.

Another way the PPL can be useful is as a convenient reminder of what you really like to do. Sometimes we get so caught up in the various "chores of life" that we forget to enjoy ourselves. By putting the PPL in a place where you'll see it often, it can softly help you to remember the direction you want to go. In addition, seeing what causes you "pain" can serve to remind you about areas of life you'd possibly like to change. If your list boldly declares that you spend 160 hours a month at a job you don't like, then it might help motivate you to look for another job.

Ultimately, to change your life, you need to change individual behaviors. If there's a lot of pain and little pleasure in your life, ask yourself the following two questions:

1) Are there any activities on the "pain" side of the list that I can easily change, do less of, or have someone else do instead?

2) Are there any activities on the "pleasure" side of the list that I can easily do more of, beginning with scheduling time for it in my life right now?

As you ask yourself these two questions, search your lists for answers you can immediately act upon. Then take action. Schedule a fun activity into your busy week, or see if you can get someone else to do what you always hate doing. Even a small change can snowball into a major shift in your attitude and disposition. Let the Pain and Pleasure List be your caring companion—gently reminding you of the road to greater fulfillment.

3. How to Easily Feel Inspired

The Magical Movie List

The TV and newspapers blare out an endless stream of bad news. Our own lives are filled with a constant barrage of stress. With so much negative information overwhelming us at all times, we need an easy and effective way to replenish our souls. Fortunately, a quick and powerful source of inspiration is readily available—movies. A good movie or video is truly a remarkable gift of modern technology. In about two hours you can enter a whole new world and become absorbed into its story, characters, and underlying message. When a movie touches your heart, it can inspire you to new heights of hope and possibility. It can almost instantly change your attitude and how you feel.

Nowadays, the average American spends about eleven years of their life watching TV—more than any other waking activity, including work! While watching TV can be fun and relaxing at times, the preponderance of violent images and bad news on TV can also be stress inducing. In fact, studies show that most people actually feel *worse* after they watch TV. On the other hand, an inspiring movie can have an uplifting effect on people for many hours—or even days. Research indicates that traits such as kindness and bravery are increased in moviegoers after they watch movies whose characters display such qualities.

Since what we watch on TV or in the movies affects how we feel and act, it's critical we become selective about what we expose ourselves to. When you were young, your parents probably prevented you from seeing certain TV shows and movies. Now that you're an adult, *you* need to choose which images and stories will help feed the type of person you want to become. Because there is a lot of "garbage" in the media, it's not an easy job to do. To help make the task easier for you, I have come up with a list of thirty highly inspiring movies. This list was created by asking approximately 2,000 people who attended my workshops about the "most inspiring movie they ever saw." The thirty movies that got the most votes ended up on the list. In alphabetical order, here are the movies most people selected:

1. *Babette's Feast*
2. *Being There*
3. *Braveheart*
4. *Brother Sun, Sister Moon*
5. *Casablanca*
6. *Chariots of Fire*
7. *Dead Poets Society*
8. *The Empire Strikes Back*
9. *E. T.*
10. *Forrest Gump*
11. *Field of Dreams*
12. *Ghandi*

13. *Gone with the Wind*
14. *Groundhog Day*
15. *Harold and Maude*
16. *Heart and Souls*
17. *Michael*
18. *Midnight Express*
19. *Mindwalk*
20. *Network*
21. *Out of Africa*
22. *Philadelphia*
23. *Powder*
24. *The Razor's Edge*

25. *Resurrection*

26. *Rocky*

27. *Schindler's List*

28. *The Ten Commandments*

29. *Titanic*

30. *The Wizard of Oz*

Of course, there are many inspirational movies that didn't make it onto this list. Yet if you haven't seen several of these movies, my advice is that you see them. Simply call your local video store and see if they carry the ones you haven't seen. A truly wonderful movie is a blessing. It can make your heart soar, teach you new ways to live, and help you gain the wisdom of the characters portrayed in the script. Not bad for about two bucks. Even if you've seen most of the movies on the above list, rent and see them again. I've learned that I often get more benefit from seeing a movie a second, third, or fourth time, than I did the first time I saw it.

A few years ago, I went to a showing of the classic movie *Harold and Maude*. The first time I saw this movie, I loved it. I was now seeing it for the fifth time. I casually commented to the woman sitting next to me that I had seen this movie on four previous occasions. She looked at me as if I was crazy, and then said, "I've seen this movie twenty-six previous times!" She was serious. She went on to tell me that this movie had totally changed her life. The main character in the movie, Maude, inspired her to leave her loveless marriage, travel around the world, and become an artist. I was amazed. Ever since I heard this woman's story, I have been much more open about the potential effects a movie can have on a person's life. Nowadays, I often see the same movie on several occasions. I've learned to "absorb" what inspires me about a particular movie so that it never seems "old." For me, watching movies has become a powerful source of illumination and learning.

In an attempt to always have new stimulation and entertainment, we often fail to get the deeper significance of what is right in front of us. What movies have truly inspired you in the past? Perhaps it's time to see them again. What movies have simply given you a good laugh or made you feel good? With an open mind, you can watch a great movie over and over again and be nourished from it with each viewing. Like a good friend, a good movie can repeatedly feed your soul and uplift your heart.

4. How to Be Filled with Energy

The Magic Pill

Have you ever felt depressed and filled with enormous amounts of energy at the same time? Probably not. When we have a lot of energy, we both feel better and get more done. Of course, we're told that the way to greater vim and vigor is to eat right, exercise, and avoid harmful substances. We know what we *should* do, but we often don't have the energy or discipline to follow through. If you're like me, you wonder "are there any safe shortcuts to having more energy?" Luckily, there are. There are now a plethora of supplements you can buy in health food stores that can safely and effectively supply your body with more vitality. Once you find one that works well for you, it's like finding a magic pill that helps you feel healthier, happier, and more energized. Who knows, you may even become motivated to eat better and exercise more often!

If you go to a health food store and ask about supplements to give you more energy, you'll likely be overwhelmed by the number of products available. After much trial and error, I've learned three things about how to find the right supplement for your body. First of all, it's important to look at the ingredients in each of the bottles. Many energy supplements are really just caffeine-like derivatives that take a toll on your body. Caffeine, Ma Huang, Ephedra, and Guarana are all very similar in that they stress your adrenal glands and ultimately leave you with less energy. It's better to look for products whose main ingredients are things like bee pollen, spirulina, wheat grass, amino acids, ginseng, blue green algae, royal jelly, or vitamin B-12.

The second thing helpful to know when looking for a supplement is that different pills work for different people. Just because your friend swears that Product X changed her life doesn't mean it will have any effect on you. It's best to buy small amounts of several products and give each one a trial run to see which one works best. In addition, you may need to try each supplement for a month or so to notice what, if anything, it does for you. Thirdly, there's a tendency for your body to gain a "tolerance" for whatever you take. This means that, over time, it has less effect on your body. That's why it may take more caffeine than it used to in order for you to feel really "buzzed." If you've tried several supplements, you can begin with the one that had the greatest effect, but periodically change to others when you feel you're building up a tolerance.

Bearing all this in mind, there are several supplements I can heartily recommend because of their ingredients and the consistently good results people report. My personal favorite is something called Uptime. Although it has a small amount of caffeine in it, it has plenty of nutritional goodies that more than make up for the fact that it contains a little caffeine. If you're a coffee drinker, definitely consider using Uptime as a healthier alternative. If you can't find it in your health food store, you can order it directly by calling (800) 441-5656.

Another favorite is something called *Ultra Energy Plus* by the Rainbow Lite company. This product is filled with good stuff and contains no caffeine at all. Although it doesn't take effect as quickly as Uptime, it can give you a nice boost of sustained energy. Think of it as a powerful food that blasts your body with vitamins. For people who like to take only natural herbs instead of vitamins, there's a product called Herbal Uprising. It's especially suitable for people who are very sensitive to supplements.

There are also various drinks you can buy to give your body a boost of energy. Nowadays there are many places that offer a variety of fresh squeezed juices that are energizing and good for you. Look for smoothies that have bee pollen, vitamin B-12, or a lot of "green stuff" added to them, or try some fresh wheatgrass juice. A big smoothie sipped throughout the day can provide you with plenty of vitamins and sustained energy. Experiment with what your local juice bar offers until you find one that tastes good and feels great.

The great thing about finding a magic pill or drink that lifts you up is how easy it is. No matter how lazy you are, you can always pop a pill into your mouth or drink some fresh juices. Although supplements are easy to "use," their effect can be life transforming. Many people don't realize that the reason they feel depressed or unhealthy is due to a lack of nutrients. I've seen clients in my therapy practice who literally change overnight by finding a supplement they really needed to take. Once you find one or two things that feel good to your body, you'll have a consistent way to support your body, mind, and spirit. With a little exploring, for under a dollar a day, you can find a supplement that can have a major impact on your life. That's a deal too good to refuse.

5. How to Neutralize Bad News

Asking About What's Good

*I*f your life is anything like mine, several times a week you receive what appears to be "bad news." It need not be anything big. Perhaps you realize that your car needs a new muffler or your back begins to ache again. Since things often don't go the way we want, it's important to learn to handle life's little upsets without losing one's equanimity. How can that be done? One approach is to try to look on the bright side of whatever happens in your life. That sounds good in theory, but it can be difficult to do in the real world of constant activity and stress. What's needed is a simple technique that can quickly change our thinking—even though we feel upset. That's no small task. Luckily, there's a method that is so simple and effective that it has even worked for a lazy person like myself. I call it "Asking About the Good."

A few years back, I was giving a lecture on how good things can come from seemingly disturbing problems. During the break, a student approached me and said he had something for me in his car. As he took his time rummaging through his car, I got increasingly annoyed because I was taking too much time away from class. Every time I was about to head back to class, he'd say, "Wait! I think I found it." Finally, I insisted I must get back to class. As I entered the class, about 100 people yelled, "Surprise!" It was the day after my birthday, and most of my friends had come to throw me a party.

What was humbling about this experience was the fact that I had just been talking about seeing the positive in adversity, but had totally missed the opportunity when it happened. I realized that in order to feel peace during difficult times, a very simple and precise technique was needed. The idea alone is not enough to help when the crap is hitting the fan. Therefore, I tried various methods that I thought would help. Most failed miserably, but one technique has withstood the test of time and challenge. Whenever a problem arises, I simply ask myself, *What could potentially be good about this?* Then, even if I don't believe it, I come up with at least two things that could *potentially* be valuable about the problem I'm facing. If nothing else, when difficulties arise in my life, they can always help me learn important inner traits such as compassion, patience, humility, and faith.

The question "What could potentially be good about this?" is a great aid to gaining equanimity in life. Besides the fact that it takes your mind off the negative aspects of the situation at hand, it can help you see the possible opportunities that were invisible to you before. Most growth, whether it be personal or professional development, comes from facing challenges and turning them into opportunities. If you can sincerely ask yourself the above question when you're upset or stressed, you can quickly find your way back to a feeling of peace.

When asking yourself "What could potentially be good about this?" you need not come up with answers you truly believe. Just the simple act of inventing a couple of possibilities will help you to feel better. Normally, when something happens that we don't like, we don't see *anything except* what made us upset. We lose all perspective.

Imagine you have a black dot the size of a nickel on the page in front of you. If your eyeball were right on top of that black dot, all you would see is black. A person in such a position would rightfully state, "I see nothing but a big black void, devoid of any color. That's all there is out here—total darkness." When you ask about the potential good of any situation, it helps you to gain perspective once again. It points your mind away from the black dot, and towards the bigger page of your life. Even if you aren't convinced that anything good could come from the problem at hand, at least you're no longer glued to the black dot. The experience of inner peace results from the ability to see that any "black dot" is only a small part of the picture of life. From a yard away, a nickel-sized dot is no big deal; from across the room, it's hardly noticeable.

The best way to see how well this method works is to try it out. Fortunately, life will give you many opportunities! Let's say that you come home one day and find that your neighbors have a new dog—one that has a predilection for barking for no apparent reason. After hearing the dog bark for two hours straight, you feel like hurting someone. Instead, you ask, "What could potentially be good about this?" At first you exclaim, "Nothing!" Yet, you know that such thinking won't do you any good, so you strain to come up with two possibilities. First, you think, "Well, I'll have to talk with my neighbors about this, and potentially we could become closer as we work out the problem." You're halfway there. Finally, you begrudgingly think, "I guess this is motivating me to communicate my needs, and better stand up for myself—which I often find hard to do." Now that your thinking is not stuck on the black dot, you can see how this situation can be used for your growth. Congratulations! Besides turning this situation into a growth opportunity by asking a simple question, you will most likely also feel a bit better.

It can be hard to remember to ask about the good when you're upset. In addition, even when you remember to ask, it might be hard to come up with two answers. You'll probably notice that there's a part of you that actually resists looking on the positive side. Yet there's no joy or energy in the experience of feeling "woe is me." By asking about the potential good, you'll soon feel better and be better at solving life's little upsets. As you learn to use this method as a habitual response to problems, you'll develop confidence that any situation can be turned into an opportunity for your growth. When you can consistently see the "silver lining" in the upsets of life, you'll be well on your way to creating lifelong happiness.

6. How to Get High without Drugs
The Power Breath

*A*s a student of various forms of yoga and meditation, I've tried many ways of "getting high" without abusing my body with harmful drugs. Throughout my years of practice, I was always on the lookout for methods that could be done quickly, and yet have a very definite effect. I came upon the Power Breath while at an ashram in India, and it promptly became my favorite breathing technique. The beauty of this method is that it only takes ninety seconds to do, and yet it's energizing effect can last for an hour. In addition, it can drastically change how you feel, propeling you from a lethargic feeling all the way to euphoria in under two minutes. Sound interesting? Then read on.

To do the Power Breath, sit up in a chair with your spine straight. Make a soft fist out of each hand, and place the back of your hands so they're near your shoulders. Have a clock or stop watch in front of you so you can easily check when a full minute has passed. To begin the breath, inhale powerfully through your nose while lifting your arms straight over your shoulders. When you exhale, bring your hands back next to your shoulders as you powerfully let out air through your nose. That's it. Repeat this form of aerobic breathing as quickly and as intensely as you possibly can for a full sixty seconds. If you need to slow down due to lightheadedness, take a regular deep breath, then proceed once again at a comfortable pace. The more powerfully and rapidly you do each breath, the more effect you'll likely feel.

Once you've done this breath for the full minute (which will seem like a very long time), take one last deep breath and hold it. You can put your hands in a comfortable position on your lap. Hold your breath for at least twenty seconds, and longer if you can. Then, exhale with a long, slow sighing sound. Aaahhhhhhhhhh! Feel the energy throughout your body. Pretty amazing, isn't it?

While your body is in this energized and relaxed state, it can be helpful to think of something you're looking forward to doing in your life. It can be a small thing, such as a good meal, seeing your partner or kids, or anything else that occurs to you. The combination of having an energized body and a mind focussed on positive things will help you to feel particularly good. Sit for as long as you like in this state of mind. If you have things you need to do, you'll now be in a better frame of mind to do them. If you have some time, simply enjoy the feeling of euphoria that often results from this form of breathing.

Besides the immediate physical and psychological effects of this breath, it's also incredibly good for you. The Power Breath is a quick way to oxygenate the blood and help your body get rid of toxins. You may find that it's initially hard to do with any amount of speed or intensity, but if you do it every day for a month, you'll notice a tremendous difference. You'll feel more energy, healthier, and more relaxed.

There are a couple of added things that are helpful to be aware of when doing the Power Breath. First, don't do it after a meal. It will just make you nauseous. Second, if you can't breathe well through your nose, it's okay to inhale and exhale through your mouth. In addition, before doing the exercise, it's a good idea to blow your nose so it's easier to breathe. And thirdly, a minute is longer than you think. If you can set an alarm to go off in a minute, that will save you from having to constantly look at the time. Instead, you can close your eyes and focus on your breath. After you feel comfortable doing this exercise for sixty seconds, try doing it for even longer periods of time. The longer you do it for, the more energy you're likely to experience in your body.

The Power Breath requires nothing except you, air, and a couple of minutes. That's its beauty. You can use it to change your mood, feel more energy, become relaxed—even to replace a cigarette or candy bar. If it causes lightheadedness when you first try it out, simply slow down your breathing. It only means your body isn't used to getting so much oxygen. By continuing to practice this breath, you'll soon notice you feel stronger than before, and your dizziness will disappear. Instead of power lunches or workouts, you'll become hooked on the Power Breath. Since wherever you go you always take your breath with you, it will be a nice friend to have.

7. How to Stop Worrying About Money

The Not-Enough Antidote

One of the reasons most people give for feeling unhappy is that they simply don't have enough money. If the money you currently have could assume a human form and talk to you, what might it say? If you're like most people, it would probably say something like this: "You never appreciate me. All you ever do is complain about how I'm never enough.

You're always worrying about how I might let you down in the future, or might leave you. I feel like you don't trust me at all. And after all I do for you! I'm always getting things for you, protecting you, entertaining you, and making your life easier—but do I ever get a heart-felt thank you? Nooooo!" If we treated our mate the way we "relate" to money, he or she wouldn't want to hang around us!

Trying to get "enough" money can be like trying to fill a gigantic bowl in which, no matter how much stuff you put into the bowl, it never fills up. We put a Mercedes in the bowl, a new house, a boat, but it never seems full for more than a few minutes. The reason the bowl never fills up is because it has a big leak in the bottom! Whatever we manage to get and put into our life, like a bowl with a leak, it quickly runs out. We are soon left completely empty.

The bowl represents our desires. We keep trying to fill this leaking bowl, enticed by television ads and movies that tell us *if we only had* (fill in the blank), *then* we'd finally be full filled. But because the bowl has a major leak in the bottom, we never get to the place where we feel we have enough. When people start having some material success, it can sometimes trigger an even bigger leak in the bowl of desires. So begins the endless cycle of never feeling really satisfied.

In my book *Real Wealth: A Spiritual Approach to Money and Work,* I talk about simple antidotes for the "not enough disease." The ability to feel thankful for what we have right now is one way to plug up the leak in the bottom of our bowl of endless desires. By feeling grateful for the things in your life, a whole new energy and experience is created. People often pursue money for years just so they can have a few moments of feeling satisfied. Yet, the practice of gratitude can make us feel rich faster than any "get-rich-quick" scheme ever invented. After all, if you feel thankful for what you have, you're immediately rich! But if you have millions and don't appreciate it, then you're *eternally* poor.

Perhaps you're thinking it would be easy to feel grateful if you only had some more money. If only, if only—the curse of the modern mind. If you own a car, you are automatically in the top 7 percent of wealth in the world. If you don't feel grateful for being in the top 7 percent of wealth, being in the top 2 percent won't make much difference. The truth is that you and I live better today than kings lived just one hundred years ago! We are blessed with being able to go to the grocery store and choose from 20,000 food items. We're blessed with inexpensive ways to enjoy music, read books, be entertained, talk to people on the phone, and even travel to distant lands. There's a lot we can feel grateful for—if we don't fall into the pothole of "if only" thinking.

I've learned that the discipline of gratitude begins by appreciating whatever you currently have—even if part of you doesn't like it. In my own battle with the "not enough" trap, I learned some tools that immediately helped me convert my feelings of scarcity to feelings of abundance and thankfulness. As I mentioned previously, an effective method is to simply ask yourself the question, "What could I feel grateful for?" When I began this practice, I came up with just intellectual answers. Yet over time I've been able to tune into the actual feeling of deep gratitude for the many wonderful things in my life. Gratitude is like a muscle that needs to be exercised. The more I've meditated on this question, the easier it has been to feel truly grateful, and less caught up in the trap of "if-only" thinking.

A second approach I've used in order to feel grateful is to compare myself to people less fortunate than I am. Years ago, when I was in a serious auto accident, I remember wondering if I had become paralyzed. As my hands and feet responded to my thoughts, I was overcome with gratitude. Several other people in the car were not so fortunate. Each day I still take time to feel great thankfulness for the use of my limbs. Many people have found it helpful to keep a "gratitude journal" in which they list five things they are grateful for each day. A daily practice such as this is useful for calming the mind and awakening an inner sense of abundance.

A third and final way to stop worrying about money is to have a written Plan B. A Plan B is simply a blueprint of what you could do if you ever experienced money troubles. When I wrote down my Plan B, I realized I had over a dozen things I could do to bail me out of financial difficulties. Seeing these ideas on paper helped me to feel assured that, if bad times ever came, I could handle it. After all, I already had a plan. Worrying about money is a nonproductive waste of energy. By feeling grateful for what you already have and having a backup plan in case of difficulties, you can greatly reduce the time you spend worrying. If you can do that, you'll feel more relaxed and peaceful. Feeling at peace and okay in the world is what real wealth is all about.

8. How to Instantly Relax

The One-Breath Technique

*I*f your life is at all like mine, it's both busy and stressful. Most people handle the onslaught of stress they face by taking periodic vacations to recover from their life. While vacations are a good idea, you can't take one every time your life becomes hectic. In addition, taking a weekend or a week off to go to Hawaii doesn't help you cope with anxiety once you're back in the rat race. What's needed is a simple way to let go of stress that can be done while you're still in the stressful situation—not five days later. That's why I created the One-Breath Technique. In twenty to sixty seconds of doing this powerful method, you can experience letting go of bodily tensions, negative emotions, and useless anxiety. It's a wonderful gift to give yourself.

I created the One-Breath Technique (OBT) when I noticed how frequently something made me impatient, uptight, or annoyed during the day. Without something to interrupt my stress, my minor upsets often snowballed into a momentum of negativity. Rather than using a technique that required taking several minutes away from the situation at hand, I saw the value of doing something right in the moment. The OBT can be done almost anywhere and, with practice, won't even be noticeable by others. Despite its brevity, it can effectively interrupt the build-up of stress and frustration that can so easily happen in modern day life.

The first step in doing the OBT is to become aware that you're stressed, upset, or could benefit from a mini-relaxation break. Next, observe the location in your body that you feel the most tightness or discomfort. For many people, they feel stress most noticeably in their shoulders, their chest, or their stomach area. Some people feel tension in many parts of their body simultaneously. Wherever you feel stress the most, imagine inhaling pure, soothing air into that area. Breathe as deeply as you can, first filling up your abdomen with air, then your chest. Once you've taken in as much air as you can, hold your breath for ten seconds.

During the time that you're holding your breath, attempt to tighten all the areas of your body that feel stressed. For example, if your shoulders are tight, tense them even more—perhaps by bringing them closer to your ears. If your stomach feels uncomfortable, tense the muscles in that area (while you hold your breath)—as if you're preparing for someone to hit you in the belly. Imagine squeezing the tension out of your body as you contract your muscles as much as you can. At the end of your ten count of tightening muscles and holding your breath, it's time for you to fully relax. Let go of your breath with a long, slow sighing sound (if you're in a place where making a sound is okay). While you're letting go of your muscles and your breath, think to yourself, "Let it all go," or some other simple phrase that works for you.

When you relax your muscles and your breath, you'll notice a warm feeling of relaxation traveling through your body. Focus on the tingling warm sensations as they move through you. Notice if there are any parts of your body that still feel tight, and if so, try to let them go as well. Although it's called the One-Breath Technique, you're welcome to do it once or twice more if you need to, and if you have the time.

There are many minor variations you can do with the OBT to make it better meet your specific affinities and needs. For instance, you might want to visualize a relaxing scene immediately following exhaling your breath. Some people find it helpful to silently hum a favorite relaxing tune after they let go of their tension. Also, if you're in a public area, you may need to be more conservative about tightening your shoulders or making a sighing sound as you exhale. As you practice this method, you'll soon notice ways to adapt it to better meet your needs and preferences.

Once again, here are the steps for doing the OBT:

1. Notice that you're feeling stressed, and become aware of where in your body you feel tight.

2. Slowly breathe in soothing air to the area you feel most tight—until you can't inhale any more.

3. When your lungs are full, hold your breath for ten seconds. During these ten seconds, tighten all the muscles in your body that feel tense, such as your shoulders, chest, and stomach area.

4. After ten seconds, exhale with a sighing sound as you completely relax all your muscles. During the exhalation, think of a phrase such as, "Let it all go." Feel the warm sense of relaxation energy as it moves through your body.

5. Repeat if necessary, or if time allows.

Part of the beauty of the OBT is its simplicity. In less than a minute, you can interrupt your stressful reactions that can lead to a bad day, bad health, and ultimately, a bad time in life. Fortunately, because it is brief and can even be invisible to the people around you, there is no good reason not to use it. In fact, why not try it right now. I mean it. If you like it, perhaps you'll get in the One-Breath habit. It's one of the healthiest habits you'll ever have. Right now would be an excellent time to begin.

9. How to Be Filled with Confidence

Power Songs and Power Moves

*T*here are two primary ways to feel confidence. The first way is to become so good at a particular skill that you can't help but feel confident. For example, you probably feel confident while tying your shoes or driving a car. Yet, because you haven't done much public speaking, you probably don't feel confident talking to large groups of people. Of course, if you spend enough time practicing, you might feel self-assured speaking to groups, but even then there's no guarantee. Besides, you may not have the time to get good at a skill before you're faced with needing to use it. Is it possible to feel confident even when you're a novice or new to a situation? Fortunately, the answer is yes. Confidence is a feeling you can learn to tap into whenever you desire simply by controlling what you think and how you use your body. Through the methods of Power Songs and Power Moves, you can learn to feel self-assured whenever you need to.

I used to be a very shy teenager. To overcome my nagging fear and self-doubt, I learned that I could sing certain songs in my head that would temporarily bolster my confidence. Before asking a woman out on a date, or presenting a talk in front of a group, I would silently sing the refrain from specific songs. I noticed that it took my mind off my fear, and instead made me feel the "energy" of the song that was "playing" in my head. For instance, if I was about to ask a woman out, I might hear the refrain, "She loves you, yeah, yeah, yeah; she loves you, yeah, yeah, yeah, she loves you—and you know that can't be bad!" Imagining the Beatles in full stereophonic sound inside my head had the effect of making me feel I couldn't lose.

Years later, I realized that I could add Power Moves to my songs, and the confidence-creating effect would be magnified. A Power Move is any way of walking, moving, or breathing that temporarily fills a person with a sense of energy and confidence. Remember the old Superman cartoons or TV show? Superman always moved in a manner that showed he was in charge. After some practice I realized that if I "pretended" I was Superman, and walked and moved like him, I began to feel unstoppable. Try it yourself. Sit up and breathe as if you were Superman, (or if you're a woman, you might try Wonder Woman). Of course, you're welcome to choose other super hero's such as Hercules or Xena, the Warrior Princess. Put a look of determination on your face as if you were a hero who has come to save the day. Now try walking with big strides like a super hero. Doesn't that feel powerful?

To experience the greatest effect from Power Songs and Moves, you need to come up with specific things that work for you. First, begin by thinking of a couple of songs that get you all fired up. All you need is a single line from a favorite song that's easy to remember. I've encouraged many of my clients to use the refrain from the Beatles song, "Revolution," where John Lennon screams, "Don't you know it's gonna be—all right!" Yet, the best song is one that feels good, fiery, and right for you. If you don't care for rock music, you might try silently "humming" a snippet from a favorite classical song. I've known many people who have used the inspiring music from the movies Rocky or Star Wars to help them tune into a feeling of confidence and power.

Once you have the right song lined up, practice different ways of moving your body so that a feeling of energy is created. Besides Power-Walking, you can practice Power-Sitting by imagining how you'd feel if you were just told you won the lottery. Through trial and error I discovered that when I take a deep breath, make a fist out of my right hand, sit up straight, put a look of determination on my face, and sing a power song, I begin to feel like I can do anything. Even if I'm about to encounter an overwhelming situation, I can easily tap into the wellspring of power within by using these methods. In fact, you might try that for yourself right now. If you do, you'll notice that in ten seconds, you'll feel totally different.

A couple of years ago, I was scheduled to be on the CNN show *Talk Back Live* for a lengthy interview. To help their guests feel more comfortable speaking in front of millions of people, the producers tell you days before the interview exactly what questions the host will ask you. Unfortunately, due to someone's error, my interviewer didn't receive the list of questions he was supposed to ask. Two minutes before I went on live to 180 countries, I was informed that we would both have to "wing it" for the full fifteen minute interview. I immediately felt a sense of panic. I remember feeling something that could only be translated as, "I want my mommy." With the two minutes I had before air time, I began singing to myself and sitting up straight like a super hero. By the time the interview began, I was completely relaxed and confident, and the interview went extremely well.

Power Songs and Power Moves are amazing tools to have at your disposal. To get the most out of them, use them with intensity. Don't just softly sing a song in your head—SCREAM IT silently to yourself like you're imitating a famous rock star. Don't simply walk or sit like you feel pretty good, move like you are completely UNSTOPPABLE! If you really allow yourself to let go and pretend, you'll soon find that it no longer feels like an act. You will feel totally self-assured. You *will* be unstoppable. And when you overcome your fear and feel a sense of confidence, you can give your very best to whatever situation is at hand. Enjoy.

Loving Yourself

*I*n recent years, a lot of books and public discussion have occurred over the issue of self-esteem. Even politicians have advocated the need to raise kids' self-esteem to ward off violence, drug use, and a host of other societal problems. Parents have been encouraged to praise their children regularly, and teachers have been admonished for criticizing kids. While I believe this focus on self-esteem is mostly a good thing, it misses a key point. Self-esteem is not something you *give* to someone else, but rather something a person *develops* through the actions they take. In this section, I will reveal eight powerful methods for learning how to love yourself. If you practice these simple exercises, you'll soon find you'll feel better about yourself, and more confident about your abilities.

There's an old saying that when you smile, the world smiles back. However, the opposite is also true. When you feel desperate and really need someone to talk to, nobody wants to be your friend. In an attempt to feel loveable, many people try to "raise" their self-esteem by impressing others. Yet, this approach almost never works. It is only when we *truly do* love and take care of ourselves that we receive the respect and admiration of the people around

37

us. When we feel secure within, it shows, and people are naturally attracted to us. Then, from our personal abundance, we can better give love and support to the people around us.

In the Western educational system, most people never learn how to tap into feelings of self worth. Therefore, many people believe that, to feel good about themselves, their only option is to "make it big" in the material world. That's why women typically spend so much time and energy trying to look beautiful, and why men are so focused on making money and being successful in their careers. While there is nothing wrong with being successful in the world, what really matters is feeling good about yourself and your life. Each of the methods presented here is a powerful way to develop a better relationship with your self. Since wherever you go you always take yourself along for the ride, it's important to learn to enjoy your own company. These tools will help you to do that.

1. How to Feel Totally Appreciated:
The Birthday/Funeral Gift

The best present you can possibly receive is the gift of love. Yet, for better or worse, love is not something you can package, sell, or put on your shelf for later use. However, there is a gift you *can* receive from your friends and family that is the next best thing. I call it the Birthday/Funeral Gift (BFG). The BFG is a gift you ask for from people who care about you. It's a present that can help you feel loved for many years to come. It can pick you up when you're feeling down, and it can send you soaring to new heights when you already feel pretty good. A good time to ask for this gift is around the time of your birthday. Most people are more than happy to give this gift because it makes *them* feel good, makes you feel good, and it doesn't cost anything except a few minutes of their time.

I came up with the idea of the Birthday / Funeral Gift when I was having my 33rd birthday. I had recently had a near death experience, and was feeling glad to be alive. I realized that I didn't need or want any material gifts, but instead I wanted the gift of feeling loved and appreciated. Therefore, I invited people who cared about me to a birthday party I was throwing for myself. I told them not to bring gifts and that I would ask them instead to share a favorite story about me at the party.

Once the party had been going awhile, I asked everyone to form a circle. I explained that, as a gift to myself, I wanted everyone to share a favorite memory about their connection with me. I pointed out that at the funeral of deceased loved ones, people usually say wonderful things about the departed. I told my friends and family that, having nearly died recently, I wanted to *know while I was still alive* what people would say about me at my funeral. After all, at my funeral all their loving comments would likely do me little good. Yet, if they said them now, I could tape record their words and listen to them in times when I needed inspiration. People were very receptive to the idea. I put my tape recorder on, laid down in the middle of the circle, and closed my eyes. Since my eyes were closed and I didn't have to speak, I could more easily be receptive to what each person had to say.

Some people spoke about me as if they were actually attending my funeral, while others spoke to me more directly. Although I expected my friends and family to say nice things about me, I was surprised to hear the depth of their appreciation and love. I was also amazed by the many personal stories they shared, and the inspiring details of what they appreciated about me. It was quite overwhelming. During the whole experience, I sat in the middle, motionless, doing my best to drink it all in as best I could.

When my Dad began speaking about me, it brought many in the room (including me) to tears. He shared how, of his three kids, he had worried about me the most. He saw how unhappy I was as a child, and was even concerned that I might kill myself as a teenager. He then poured out his heart of how proud he was of me now. He shared that he could barely believe that, through many years of working on myself, I had become a person he deeply loved, enjoyed, respected, and looked up to. His words touched my soul at a very profound level. Somewhere deep inside me, I felt like I could relax now and know that I was fully loved.

After everyone had a turn to share a personal story or appreciation, I was invited to come back to life. I was given many hugs, and everyone felt quite high. I turned off the tape recorder, and put the cassette in a safe place. Occasionally, when I feel down or need a boost of love and confidence, I listen to the tape. It never fails to bring tears to my eyes and a dose of love to my heart.

The Birthday/Funeral Gift can be done in many different ways. It is not necessary that all your friends and family gather in one place in order to benefit from this gift to yourself. An easy alternative is to write a letter to people you love explaining what you would like from them. Tell them that you're looking for a story of appreciation and/or what they would say about you at your funeral. It's a good idea to briefly explain why you want this, and how you will use it as a loving gift to yourself in times of need. In your letter, tell your friends and family in what form you would prefer their contribution, letter, fax, e-mail, or on a cassette tape. Give them plenty of time to respond before your birthday. If you desire, you can read (or listen) to them all at once, or savor each one as they arrive at your house.

The Birthday/Funeral Gift is perhaps the best present you will ever receive. Unlike the possessions we typically get as gifts, this present can impact you for many years. It can show you that you really *do* matter in the lives of other people. It can inspire you to give your love and share your gifts with loved ones—knowing that such things are always noticed and appreciated. The love you feel for others, and the caring they feel for you, shouldn't wait until tragedy hits. Let the healing words and affection flow now, while you and your loved ones can still soak it in. Let this new form of birthday gift help inspire and heal you—or someone you love.

2. How to Grow Your Self-Esteem

Mirror, Mirror on the Wall

*I*n the movie *Snow White*, the queen asks her mirror who is the "fairest one of all." The mirror breaks the bad news to her that there is someone much more beautiful than she.

Like the queen, most of us have bought the idea that we are not as beautiful, worthy of love, or as good as someone else. Capitalizing on our insecurities and lack of self-worth, advertisers tell us that if we were only richer or more beautiful, we'd be loved. Although we may know better in theory, it's easy to fall into the trap of trying to gain recognition from others as a *substitute* for our lack of self-love. Yet, there is no substitute for really liking yourself. Even if the whole world applauds you, if you don't feel good about yourself, it doesn't matter. Unfortunately, the sad truth is that most people *don't* feel good about themselves. Therefore, what's needed is a practical and powerful way to grow our sense of self-worth. Fortunately, there is a method that can greatly nurture and enhance a person's sense of self-esteem. I call it the Mirror Exercise (ME).

To do the Mirror Exercise, simply go to a mirror, (or find a hand held one), and look your self in the eyes. Notice what thoughts or feelings come up for you. Then, begin talking to your self out loud, as if you were talking to a really good friend. Tell the person in the mirror how much you care and appreciate him or her. Acknowledge what you're proud of. Say things that the person in the mirror needs to hear in order to feel accepted and cared for. Imagine that you're talking to a young, vulnerable child who needs to be encouraged. Here's what your "conversation" might sound like:

"Hello Jonathan. How are you? You've been feeling pretty stressed lately, haven't you? Well, you've been busy helping a lot of people. You need to remember to take care of yourself. You deserve it. You've worked hard. It's amazing all the tasks you do. I'm proud of the fact that you've become a very giving person over the years. I appreciate how you're really committed to helping others. I like you. You're often a lot of fun to be with. Some of the stories you said last night at the party were really funny. I appreciate your sense of humor. You don't have to try so hard to be liked—because you *are* liked. Not for what you do, but for who you are. I want you to know that you're doing just fine. Allow yourself to relax more and just receive all the goodwill people feel towards you. I respect who you are, and I want you to know I love you."

Although there is no formula for what to say during this exercise, it's helpful if you steer clear of put-downs. If you notice you begin to think of negative judgments during the ME, tell those thoughts, "Thank you for sharing, but right now I'm committed to loving myself." You may find this exercise difficult to do at first, but it becomes easier with practice. It's common for negative thoughts to arise, especially when you are complementing yourself. As you practice this exercise, you'll notice that the self-criticisms fade more into the background, and the self-appreciations are taken in at a deeper level. After awhile, you'll begin to feel a deep love and compassion for the person in the mirror.

There are many variations to the basic ME that can be tried for different effects. For example, you may try to do this exercise completely naked in front of a full-length mirror. Most people are at war with their bodies, but the ME can help. By starting with specific parts of your body that you like, you can eventually get to accept *every* part of your anatomy. During this form of the Mirror Exercise, talk to the various parts of your body and try to develop a better relationship with them. For example, you might say, "Hello nose. As you know, you're bigger than I would like you to be, but I am grateful for all the wonderful smells you send my way. I'm going to try to appreciate you more. You really do a great job. Thank you for adding to my life."

If you have favorite affirmations you use for your growth, saying them while you look in the mirror is a way to "turbo-charge" their effect on you. The simple affirmation, "I am committed to loving you and taking care of you" is a powerful statement to say to yourself. Because the Mirror Exercise is so effective, there is often a lot of resistance to doing it. You may feel squeamish, silly, or stupid at first. In general, feelings of embarrassment or resistance are all signs that you could greatly benefit from this method. At first, the ME can bring to the surface how difficult it is for you to feel or express love for yourself. Yet with practice, those initial feelings of armoring will get peeled off like layers of an onion. You'll soon be left with a loving relationship with yourself. When you look into the mirror, you'll no longer hear a critical voice saying how you're not good enough. Instead, you'll appreciate that you are an absolutely perfect rendition of yourself.

3. How to Encourage Yourself

The Art of Adult Rewards

When you were a child, your parents most likely rewarded you on a fairly regular basis. Perhaps they told you how pretty you were, or bought you an ice cream cone as a reward for cleaning the yard. However they did it, the rewards you received helped guide you, and made you feel loved. Unfortunately, once you left your parent's home, there was probably no one around to play the role of encourager and guide for you. The truth is—if you don't do it for yourself, it probably won't get done. As adults, we need to learn how to give *ourselves* rewards so we can be encouraged to move in a positive direction. However, most adults either give themselves indulgences *all* the time, or they almost *never* do. By learning the art of giving ourselves rewards at *appropriate* times, we can come to benefit from this powerful tool.

The first and perhaps hardest task in learning to encourage yourself is to come up with a *list* of at least a dozen rewards. What are *rewards*? Basically, they are anything that you enjoy doing or having. The best treats are ones that are not harmful to your health, are readily available, and don't cost much. That means that a week-long trip to Paris is a nice idea, but it wouldn't be good to put on your list. You can ask yourself, "What are little things I like to do or have that I rarely treat myself to?" After asking myself that question, I came up with the following list:

1. Taking a bath.

2. Listening to my favorite music for a half hour.

3. Eating chips and salsa.

4. Going to a movie.

5. Going to my favorite nearby nature spot.

6. Calling one of my friends that lives on the East coast.

7. Playing guitar.

8. Getting a professional massage or a brief one from my partner.

9. Watching a favorite TV show.

10. Going to a favorite restaurant.

11. Being physically intimate with my partner.

12. Reading the newspaper.

Notice some of the items on my list cost money, and some don't. Some involve other people, while others don't. Certain items can be done in five minutes, while others might take an entire evening. It's good to have a variety of items on your list so you can have different levels and types of rewards. Once you've made your list, put a copy of it in a place where you'll see it often. People frequently forget to reward themselves for hard work. If you have your list in a prominent place, it will help remind you that you need to take care of yourself.

With your rewards list done, you can now begin using it to shape your behavior. The first thing you can do is ask yourself, *"What would I like to encourage and motivate myself to do?"* Think of a few key behaviors that you know you *should* do, but often avoid doing. Perhaps it's exercising regularly, contacting new clients at work, or meditating every day.

Whatever it is, you can decide to give yourself an appropriate reward *after* you do what is difficult for you to do. For large tasks, such as finishing a major project at work, you might give yourself a sizeable prize. For small tasks, consider giving yourself just a small, simple treat. After a while, your brain will get the message that it's worth doing difficult tasks because you invariably get rewarded for your efforts.

In my therapy practice, my clients and I often make "deals" in which they agree to give themselves a major reward once they've achieved a specific goal. For example, I had a client named Frank who had always wanted to go on a trip around the world. He made a deal with me that as soon as he had $20,000 saved up, he would immediately buy his tickets and go. Although at the time he made the deal he had almost no money, he managed to save the full amount in a mere eighteen months. Dangling a big enough carrot in front of your self can create miraculous changes in your behavior and abilities.

Some people are used to giving themselves rewards all the time. They eat big meals, go to movies, and take nice trips as an everyday occurrence in their life. If you're like that, then you might consider giving yourself your "normal rewards" only *after* you've done something you know would be good for you to do. Each person must find a healthy balance between doing work and receiving rewards. If you tend to be a workaholic, be sure to treat yourself to something pleasurable after each difficult task you complete. If you tend to be indulgent, make your access to rewards dependent on completing some of your responsibilities.

A loving parent knows when their child needs encouragement, and when they need to be disciplined. Now that you're all grown up, you need to decide for yourself what you need. With practice, you'll find the right amount of rewards that help you feel motivated, supported, and balanced in life.

4 How to Stop Putting Yourself Down

Getting Bertha off Your Back

When I was in my early teen years, I barely spoke. People considered me to be painfully shy. However, the real reason I didn't talk was because I was a slave to someone known as Bertha. Bertha would scream at me whenever I attempted to make friends with anyone. In a voice full of alarm and panic, she would yell, "You better *not* do that—you'll look stupid!" When I heard her, I would immediately back off and lose my opportunity to make a friend. The fact that Bertha was only a voice inside my own head didn't make her any less scary. She was completely in control—until I came upon a method that got her off my back, and out of my head. Once her attempts to scare me no longer worked, my life radically changed.

Most people have their own particular form of "Bertha." It may be a voice in their head that tells them they're not good enough, or smart enough, or that they'll always be a loser. Like an out of control cancer, destructive thoughts such as this can ruin a person's life if they're not attended to. The first step to handling such harmful voices in one's head is to clearly identify them. While we all have critical thoughts from time to time, most people have one or two thought patterns that are particularly destructive and limiting. Can you think of what *yours* are?

From my many years as a psychotherapist, I learned that people are often subject to similar destructive thoughts. Below is a list of ten thought patterns that often give people problems:

1. I should just kill myself.

2. I hate myself.

3. I can't do anything right.

4. No one could ever love me.

5. I better not say anything because I'll just look foolish.

6. I'm so ugly (or fat).

7. I'm so stupid.

8. She (or he) is going to pay for what they did to me.

9. I can't believe I did that. I am so dumb.

10. I just need a stiff drink (or smoke, etc.) and everything will be okay.

Once you recognize a specific destructive thought pattern from your own life or the above list, it's helpful to give it a name. My apologies to all women named "Bertha." To me, the name "Bertha" symbolizes a very fat, mean woman with a nasty temper. That's how the voice in my head said, "You better not do that, you'll look stupid!" To help me create some distance from that voice, I called it Bertha. Now that the voice was named, it didn't seem quite so ominous. After all, it was no longer *me* saying I needed to behave a certain way—it was mean and nasty *Bertha*. What is a name you could give to a specific voice in *your* head? Any name will do. The important thing is that you know precisely the thought pattern the name corresponds to. Once you've identified a specific voice and given it a name that fits, you're ready to go to battle.

The only way destructive thoughts can impact our lives is when we take them very seriously. Harmful thoughts literally feed off of our reaction to them. If we can laugh at them, or even ignore them, they soon wither away and die. They have no power other than the energy we give them. Therefore, once a person has a destructive thought identified, they need to practice ways of distancing themselves from the harmful voice. There are two simple ways of doing this. The first it to have a dialog with the destructive thought pattern, and the second is to make it seem ridiculous.

When having a dialog with your own brand of "Bertha," imagine that her job is to annoy and control you, whereas *your* job is to not take its ranting so seriously. Talk to this voice, either out loud or inside your head. Say things like, "Hello, I was expecting you now. Blah, blah, blah—you always say the same old stuff. You're going to need new material if you expect to hook me like you have in the past. Why don't you just calm down and take your finger off the panic button? Everything is just fine—you just sound stupid when you get so hysterical. You're not needed now." Of course, *your* dialog with your harmful voice should be whatever works for you. In general, the more your "Bertha" realizes you're hip to its ways, the more it will leave you alone.

The second way to get Bertha off your back is to change the tone of the voice in which she speaks to you. When I question people about the bothersome voices in their head, they almost always say they hear a mean, scary, or urgent tone of voice. In fact, much of the impact of such thoughts come from not only *what* they say, but *how* they sound. Fortunately, you can easily change the tone of the voice to sound ridiculous. Next time you hear your particular brand of "Bertha," try to say "her" thoughts using Mickey Mouse's tone of voice. If Mickey doesn't work for you, try Daffy Duck or Bugs Bunny. No matter what you think, it's hard to take it too seriously if you hear it in a Bugs Bunny tone of voice.

As you talk back to your Bertha, or change her tone of voice to sound funny, you'll no longer find her to be so scary or bothersome. Sticks and stone may break your bones, but passing thoughts need not hurt you if you don't take them so seriously. Once bothersome thoughts lose their power over you, you'll feel like a great burden has been lifted. You'll be free to act in ways that you previously avoided, and you'll be able to create new outcomes in your life. Getting Bertha out of your head and off your back can help you to soar to new heights in your life.

5. How to Avoid Freaking Out

The Art of Showering

Have you ever had a mental "freak-out?" Most people have. Our minds can sometimes fall victim to thoughts that spin out of control, resulting in a feeling of high anxiety and overwhelm. Unfortunately, once a freak-out begins, it can be hours or even days till rationality and good judgement prevail. To avoid this needless suffering, it's important to know how to quickly stop your thoughts and emotions from spiraling out of control. Historically, many people have turned to drugs or alcohol in times of great stress. Yet, that just makes matters worse. After much trial and error, I've found that the simple act of taking a shower, coupled with asking myself a simple question can help cut short even the worse freak-out experiences.

When I first became a therapist, I had a client named Linda who periodically became overwhelmed by the demands of her life. Whenever this happened, she would drink her way into oblivion, or seriously consider suicide. After a couple of suicide attempts, she sought my professional help. Linda wanted to avoid anti-depressant medication because normally she wasn't depressed. In fact, she was often quite happy—but would occasionally become subject to intense feelings of fear. I suggested that, upon the first symptoms of feeling highly stressed or having suicidal thoughts, she make her way to the nearest shower. I instructed her to begin with a warm shower, then gradually make it cooler and cooler until it was very cold. Finally, I told her to end the experience by making the water very warm. I said that a simple ten-minute shower like this can powerfully change how she thinks and feels.

Linda tried my suggestion the next time she felt overwhelmed, and was amazed at the results. However, she told me that after a few hours, the fearful thoughts returned. After all, the stressful situations in her life still existed. To avoid freaking out again, I suggested that once she dried off from the shower, she write an answer to the following question: *What are three small steps I can take to better handle the things going on in my life?"* The next week when Linda returned to my office, she exclaimed, "It worked!" Since "creating" this dual approach to handling feelings of overwhelm, I've used it with dozens of clients. They have all found it to be a practical and effective way to feel they are back in charge of their life.

The reason the showering and the "three small steps" question are so potent has to do with how we create the emotions we feel. Basically, our feelings are the result of sensations in our body combined with the focus of our mind. When we feel overwhelmed, it usually stems from trying to focus on *all* the problems we have or all the things we need to do. Inevitably, this leads to a feeling of stress in our body. Unfortunately, like a microphone caught in a feedback loop, the tightness of our body can lead to focusing even more on the problems we face. Soon, our emotions can be wailing out of control. Fortunately, this unpleasant cycle can be avoided. Showering relaxes your body and changes the focus of your mind.

Since each person reacts to stress in different ways, it's important to know the *first* signs that your emotions are careening into trouble. Ask yourself, "In previous times when I've felt overwhelmed, what were the *first* signs I was losing control?" Write your answer down on paper. This will help you recognize when to head for the shower. It's easier to kill a monster when it's small. Once in the shower, going from warm, to cold, to hot water helps to "flush" your emotions through your body, leaving you feeling relaxed and renewed. After the shower, simply get a piece of paper and write down the "anti-overwhelm" question at the top:

What are three small steps I can take to better handle the things going on in my life? Write down anything that occurs to you—just get it out of your head and onto the paper, but make sure you have at least three things.

Once you have a list of small actions you can take to handle the stress in your life, prioritize them. Ask yourself, "What's the most important thing to handle first?" Then, keep prioritizing them until you have a list of action steps, from most to least important. Finally, when you feel ready, take care of the first item on your list. By taking action, you'll feel better. You'll get out of your thinking mind and into taking care of the situation at hand. The experience of being overwhelmed results from a lot of thinking and little or no action. As you do even small steps to improve the situations at hand, you'll feel back in charge.

Sometimes people are so good at avoiding a problem that they don't even know a situation is overwhelming to them. To avoid unpleasant feelings, they stay in denial, or distract themselves a thousand different ways. For example, I had a client named Mark who had been in a very destructive relationship with his wife for a long time. Yet, he avoided ever trying to improve the relationship because, any time he thought about it, he felt inundated by fear. I suggested he try the "shower/three small steps" technique during the week to see what would happen. I told him he didn't even have to do any of the steps, he should just write them down. To his pleasant surprise, Mark not only wrote down five small things he could do, but he acted on three of them. When he excitedly walked into my office the next week, he reported, "I now have some hope. While our relationship still needs a lot of help, it feels a hundred percent better than it did last week."

If you live with people, ask them to remind you to use this method the next time you seem out of sorts. When you can quickly turn your fear into positive action, you'll avoid a lot of needless suffering, and you'll be well on your way to a happier and healthier life.

6. How to Safely Handle Your Anger

The Adult Temper Tantrum

It's been one of "those days." Too much to do, and no time to do it. Your boss yells at you for something that wasn't even your fault. By the time you make it home, you're fed up and stressed out. You slam the door, then walk past your partner without saying a word. Your mate asks you about your day and why you slammed the door. Just the fact that they say *anything* to you makes you even more annoyed. You tell them, "I didn't slam the door. There's nothing wrong. Why do you always have to question me?" You spend the rest of the evening upset.

Sound familiar? Some people play out scenes like this on a fairly regular basis. During the day, some event or person makes them angry, and they spend the rest of the day and evening affected by it. Although the original upset has long gone, they carry the residue of the event with them like a bag of bricks on their shoulders. Without a clearly defined way to rid themselves of their irritation, they spend many hours feeling annoyed for no apparent reason. Then, seemingly out of nowhere, they "blow-up" in reaction to just about anything.

It doesn't need to be like this. Think of how infants react when they get angry. Typically, they get very upset, scream or cry for awhile, then quickly return to a state of contentment. Instead of holding-in their feelings, they fully let them out. Once all their anger has been expressed, they feel calm and at peace once again. Unfortunately, adults have been conditioned to repress their feelings of anger and upset. Yet, like steam escaping from a heated pressure cooker, our anger and resentment leaks out. And because it is only allowed to leak out a little at a time, it can take a long while before we feel at peace once again.

As adults, we've been taught that it's not appropriate to "blow-up" or have a "temper tantrum." Yet, carrying anger around for hours or days on end is not a good solution either. What we need is a safe way to fully release our upsets and frustrations without making a fool out of ourselves. I've found two practical ways to accomplish this. The first I call the Adult Temper Tantrum (ATT), and the second I call the Raw Exercise.

In order to do an Adult Temper Tantrum, you first need a private room. A bedroom is best, but any room with pillows and privacy will suffice. As soon after a maddening event as possible, try to excuse yourself and go to a private room. Once in the room, take a pillow and hold it like you're getting ready for a pillow fight. Think of the person or situation that upset you. Picture it clearly in your mind, and breathe quickly as you feel yourself get angry once again. Then, once you're back in touch with the feelings of upset, begin to smash the pillow against the bed or floor as hard and as quickly as you can. If you have a lot of privacy, feel free to scream whatever comes to mind as you continue to beat the bed with the pillow. It only takes a couple of minutes of smashing the bed with a pillow (or your fists) before you'll feel a state of relaxed exhaustion. Then, congratulate yourself for having released all that toxic energy. Finally, end your session by thinking of one or two things you're grateful for in your life.

The ATT is unsurpassed in being able to get out a lot of anger from your system in a short period of time. By watching young kids, you can see that the full releasing of emotions helps to quickly restore a child back to a state of harmony. The same is true for you and me. Of course, as an adult you need to be more "mature" and wait to release your upset in a safe and private place. By having an ATT, in a couple of minutes you can release a lot of stress and be freed from bringing in "old emotions" into your daily life. Once the tantrum is over, it's always best to think of something you feel grateful for. This helps to soften your mood and energy so you'll be better able to return to your everyday life.

Sometimes a private room can be hard to find. If you're at your office, or running errands, getting to your bedroom may be many hours away. That's where the Raw Exercise (RE) becomes helpful. In the RE, you need not beat on anything. All you need to do is get in your car, play some loud music, and scream your anger out. If your car is parked, loud rock music can drown out your scream. If you're driving around, the music isn't as necessary, but can still be useful to help you feel less inhibited. It's called the Raw Exercise for two reasons. First, it's a way of letting your raw emotions out so they won't leak into the rest of your life. Second, when getting ready to yell, it's best to begin by saying the word "raw," and feeling the word in your gut. Then, slowly make your voice louder and louder until it ends in an all-out scream. This "building up" form of yelling is easier to do than beginning with a scream, and it helps to save your voice as well.

It is truly amazing how much anger and frustration can be released with a ten second scream. As kids can attest, screaming and hitting is the "natural" way for us to discharge our feelings. By getting into the habit of hitting your bed or screaming in your car when upset, you can avoid bringing toxic feelings into the rest of your life. The hardest part about doing these methods is being able to overcome your initial feelings of embarrassment. Yet, I've found that if you can do these techniques just once, you'll likely become hooked on how valuable they are. Your friends, partner, and co-workers will wonder why you seem so much more relaxed. Only your car and bed will know your little secret.

7. How to Overcome Minor Depression
Hooray for Hypericum

M any people suffer from symptoms of minor depression sometime in their life. Persistent sadness, lethargy, tiredness, or suicidal thoughts can all be signs that you're in the grips of depression. What can you do? Historically, the recommended treatment has been to take drugs such as Prozac or Zoloft—sometimes coupled with therapy. Yet, these medications present a problem for many people. First of all, getting a prescription and buying these medications can cost hundreds of dollars. Secondly, many people find that anti-depressant medications don't work at all or they can cause unpleasant side effects. Fortunately, an inexpensive and safe alternative to anti-depressant medications has recently become popular. It's called Hypericum—but it's better known as Saint Johnswort.

Saint Johnswort is derived from a yellow-flowered plant that has been ingested around the world for some 2,000 years. In 1994, the venerable Journal of Geriatric Psychiatry and Neurology devoted an entire issue to Hypericum. One study done with 3,250 patients suffering from mild and moderate depression found that 80 percent of them felt better, or completely free of symptoms, after four weeks. In Germany it is the leading treatment for depression, and is prescribed 25 times more frequently than Prozac. Best of all, Saint Johnswort can be picked up at your local health food store without a prescription, and costs a lot less than any anti-depressant on the market.

Although more research needs to be done on Hypericum, by all accounts it seems to be a very safe herb to ingest. Approximately 2.4 percent of those trying the herb experience side effects—ranging from restlessness to mild allergic reactions. The percentage of people who report side effects from Prozac or Zoloft is much higher. For example, approximately 20 percent of people who take Prozac experience headache, digestive difficulties and/or insomnia. While Hypericum may make some people sensitive to the sun, the absence of serious side effects is one of its biggest selling points.

If you suffer from mild or moderate depression from time to time, consider trying Saint Johnswort. The recommended dosage is 300 milligrams of Hypericum extract, containing 0.3 percent of the active ingredient Hypericin, three times a day. *It takes between one and four weeks for the herb to start working.* Since it takes awhile for this medicine to have an effect, avoid trying it in response to momentary sadness or lethargy. Yet, if you feel depressed for several weeks, there is little to risk and potentially a lot to gain from trying Saint Johnswort.

Because I'm a therapist and not a psychiatrist, I'm not able to prescribe medication. Frequently, clients would come to my office feeling depressed, but they lacked the funds to see a psychiatrist. In addition, some clients simply refused to take drugs such as Prozac because they didn't like its side effects or how it made them feel. When I heard about Hypericum, I began suggesting it to clients I thought could benefit from its use. In almost every case, glowing reports came back to me. Many of the clients who had previously taken anti-depressants reported they liked Hypericum better. Several of my clients said they experienced fewer side effects and/or found it to feel "more natural" than the previous medications they had tried.

If you try Hypericum or other anti-depressant remedies, it's important not to use them to avoid looking at important issues in your life. Depression can often be a sign that certain aspects of your life are not working. A good therapist or a good book that deals with a therapeutic approach to depression can be an important part of your recovery. The book *Feeling Good* by Dr. David Burns is a good place to start. Although psychotherapy can be expensive, it can sure beat the cost of spending the rest of your life running from yourself. If you decide to try therapy as part of your treatment, ask friends if they know of anyone they can recommend. Another option is to call several therapists and talk to each of them on the phone to see which one feels right for you.

Hypericum is not a cure-all for depression and sadness. Yet, for many people it can be an enormous help. If, after using Hypericum for four to six weeks, you don't notice any improvement, consider seeing a psychiatrist for his or her recommendation. If you keep trying new medications and/or forms of therapy, you'll eventually find something that helps. Don't give up hope. Even severely depressed people have been known to bounce back to a feeling of contentment after finding a treatment that was right for them. Good luck on your search.

8. How to Neutralize Bad Memories

The Erasure Technique

o bad memories or images ever haunt you? Do you sometimes flash back to some of the most traumatic moments of your past? For some reason, the human mind has a nasty tendency to forget important things like your mother's birthday, but is more than happy to frequently remind you of the worst events of your life. Fortunately, there's an antidote to this glitch in the human bio-computer. It's called the Erasure Technique. In a matter of a few minutes, this powerful method can virtually neutralize the bad feelings associated with almost anything you've ever experienced. I've even used it with clients who have suffered from disturbing memories for many years. Whether you want to neutralize images of a minor car accident or the hurt from the ending of a relationship, the erasure technique can make a dramatic difference in your life.

The theoretical underpinning of this method is that memories are stored in our brain in a similar way to how music is stored on a CD. Because precise information is encoded on a CD, every time you play it, it plays back the same music. But what if you took a nail and thoroughly scratched up the CD? If you tried to play it again, it wouldn't sound the same at all. In fact, your player would probably simply reject playing it. Well, in the Erasure Technique, something similar occurs. Using a precise process, we take a "nail" to your unpleasant memories and distort them until they are largely unrecognizable. Then, if you try to "play" the same memory again, your brain will either refuse to do so, or the memory will be so distorted that it will no longer have any impact on you. Voila! Your previously traumatic memory or image is neutralized.

Let's say you were once in a relationship in which your partner said something incredibly hurtful to you, then walked out of your life. Of course, your brain thinks you need to see this scene several times a month, but you'd like to move on. You decide to use the erasure method. To do the technique, you begin by creating a "movie" of the event in your mind. You imagine the disturbing scene from the beginning, all the way to the very end. Yet, instead of watching it the way you normally do, play the scene in *fast* motion. When you get to the end of the "movie," play it in fast *reverse*. See all the characters moving very quickly, just like one of those early silent films.

Once you've watched the scene in fast forward and reverse, it's time to add a few props to the "movie." Imagine each and every person in the scene to be wearing a big pair of Mickey Mouse ears on their head. Then proceed to watch the unpleasant event in fast motion—forward and reverse—once again. Next, give everyone in the movie a gigantic red "Bozo" nose along with their Mickey Mouse ears. See the whole thing again in fast motion, forward and reverse. Finally, watch it at least one more time, this time adding circus music in the background and whatever ridiculous things your imagination can dream up.

Once you've distorted the scene in these various ways, try to play your inner movie the way it used to be—the way it had tormented you before. What you'll likely notice is that ridiculous images keep "popping up" during the scene, even though you're not trying to create them. When your ex-lover appears with Mickey Mouse ears and a Bozo nose, and their voice sounds like Daffy Duck as they speak to you, it's hard to take it all so seriously. Instead of a gut wrenching feeling resulting from the memory, you'll feel pretty neutral about it. Congratulations! You've just healed yourself.

A client named Sharon came to me suffering from the fear of flying. When she was a little girl, she had been in a plane that made an emergency landing. Ever since, she was terrified of getting in any sort of plane. As luck would have it, her job required her to travel a lot. Occasionally she would "white knuckle" her way through a flight, but usually chose to drive—even if it was several hundred miles. I guided Sharon through the erasure process, focusing on both the original traumatic incident and recent times she had managed to get on a plane. She had fun picturing Mickey Mouse ears and Bozo noses on the flight attendants. She even laughed as she imagined clowns strolling down the aisles, complete with circus music, as the plane landed. As Sharon left my office, she was sure that such a simple process couldn't erase a lifetime of flying terror. Two weeks later, I got a call from her. After saying hello, Sharon told me she felt wonderfully relaxed. I asked her, "Is that unusual?" She responded, "You don't understand, I'm currently *on* an airplane, using one of those airplane phones! I feel no fear or anxiety at all. It worked!"

The Erasure Technique can be used for any sort of bothersome memory. In my private practice I've used it to help people who've suffered from flashbacks of accidents, embarrassing moments, and other negative events and memories. In almost every case, after a few minutes of using this method a single time, the memory became much less bothersome. Occasionally, clients have had to use the Erasure Technique a few times to get results, but it has always managed to help people feel better. If you have memories that still bother you, or seem to have had a lasting negative impact on you, consider "erasing" them. By becoming more free of your past, it will be easier to create the future you truly desire.

9. How to Heal What You Feel

The Sensation Meditation

When clients come into my office, they describe many types of problems. Yet, whatever their situation, they almost always complain that they feel stuck in feelings of anger, sadness, fear or hurt. In order to help my clients, I teach them something called The Sensation Meditation (SM). This meditation guides people to focus on their negative feelings in a specific manner. By fully feeling their emotions without distraction, people can move through "stuck" feelings into a place of healing. When people finish using this simple three minute meditation technique, they frequently report that their negative feelings have vanished, and that their body feels relaxed, peaceful, and at ease.

The first step in doing the Sensation Meditation is to find a comfortable chair or couch, and proceed to take a couple of slow, deep breaths. Then, scan your body and notice the most uncomfortable feeling or sensation you feel. Focus on this area of your body, and feel exactly whatever is there. For example, if you're annoyed you might notice a tightness in your chest and a warm feeling in your throat. If you're worried, you may notice a tension in your forehead muscles and shoulder blades. Ultimately, our emotions are experienced in our body as specific *sensations* such as warmth or coolness, tightness or relaxation, sharp or blunt, etc. As you notice uncomfortable sensations in your body, try to be aware of the *resistance* you have to experiencing these uncomfortable feelings. Instead of avoiding or pushing away the discomfort you feel, simply *allow* the sensations to be there. Give yourself full permission to feel whatever is going on in the present moment.

As you tune into your present time sensations and let go of resisting whatever is there, you may notice that things start to change. Ironically, it is largely our resistance to feeling negativity that allows uncomfortable feelings to stay stuck in our body. By letting go of your resistance and actually *focusing* on what you feel, the dam of stuck feelings will become like a moving river once again. To help you tune into the present sensations of your body, it can help to focus on the following questions:

1. Where in my body do I feel the most uncomfortable feelings or sensations?

2. How big of an area in my body does the core of these uncomfortable sensations cover?

3. Is this area warmer or cooler than the rest of my body? How exactly does it feel different?

4. What about this sensation do I resist or find uncomfortable?

5. Can I let go of my resistance and allow the sensations to flow through?

6. What is something I could feel grateful for or look forward to in my life?

As you go through each of these, do your best to focus on what the question points to. For example, if you're noticing how big of an area the sensations take, compare it to the size of a baseball, a basketball, or whatever seems appropriate. Except for question number six, each of these inquiries will help you be present with your body. The more current you can be with the actual sensations in your body, the more quickly and easily stuck feelings will dissipate. As you focus on these various questions, imagine you are a scientist objectively noticing the exact moment to moment sensations in your body. By the time you reach question number six, you'll probably feel rather relaxed. As you focus on what you feel grateful for or what you look forward to, allow yourself to be filled with the feeling of gratitude or excitement. Once you feel relaxed and positive, you can slowly open your eyes and enjoy your day.

While the Sensation Meditation is great for cutting through stuck feelings, it's also an excellent tool for getting over minor upsets. If you feel a bit tense or annoyed, try taking three minutes to do this meditation. I think you'll notice you'll soon feel relaxed and at ease. With practice, you can even do a shorter version of this meditation. To do this, simply take a deep breath, notice the uncomfortable sensations in your body, and then relax and allow what you feel to fully be as it is. As you stay present with these sensations, you'll soon observe that they change, and like a river, flow through you. If you do this method enough, you may even be able to do the whole process in under a minute. It can be a great way to love yourself.

The beauty of the Sensation Meditation is that it helps your feelings through a natural, organic process. Instead of trying to distract yourself from your feelings—which simply allows them to stay stuck—your feelings naturally become unstuck as you fully *feel* them. Although it can be hard to believe, it is our *resistance* to our feelings that allows negativity to stick around in our body. Even for major upsets, like the ending of a relationship or a death in the family, the Sensation Meditation can help you move through your grief at an accelerated rate. Sometimes, the feelings will briefly become more intense before they subside. That's part of the healing process, and shouldn't be resisted either.

To make this exercise easier to remember, you might want to write out the six questions from the meditation on a little note card. Another good thing to do is to record the meditation on a cassette tape and then, when you need it, listen to it on a portable cassette player. To create your own guided Sensation Meditation, simply tell yourself to "focus on what feels uncomfortable in your body." Wait a minute to give yourself time to feel what is there and time to try to let go of any resistance. Then, read the six questions into the tape recorder, remembering to pause for about twenty seconds after each one. That's all that's needed.

Most people are secretly at war with their own feelings. Besides the obvious stress this creates, it also has a tendency to keep our bad feelings around for longer than they need to be. Fortunately, the Sensation Meditation can help you become friends with your feelings, your body, and your self once again.

Improving Your Relationships

$\mathscr{I}$t seems we've entered a period of history when having a good, long-term intimate relationship is harder than ever to maintain. A man who recently came to see me for counseling confessed to me, "I wish I could communicate with my wife as well as I do with my computer." His comment struck me as funny at first, and then tragic. Unfortunately, people typically spend a lot more time learning how to properly "talk" to their computer than how to communicate with their partner or friends. Perhaps that's why the national divorce rate hovers around 50 percent, and very few people seem to be happy in their relationships.

There are various types of relationships we have in our lives, from ones that last a minute to ones that last a lifetime. Yet, in each of our relationships what we truly desire is a deeper sense of intimacy. Hidden within the word "intimacy" are instructions for creating the experience. To be close to someone, you must share who you really are: "in to me see." By learning skills that foster safety and trust in our relationships, we can consistently create the love we yearn for. In this section, you'll learn powerful methods for connecting with people instantly, as well as tools for maintaining loving long-term relationships. You'll discover simple ways to deepen any relationship, repair trust when it's been broken, and successfully deal with difficult people. You'll even learn a method for easily solving problems with your mate, co-workers, and family members. The tools in this part of the book can make all your relationships more harmonious, intimate, and fun.

1. How to Never Argue Again

The Art of Spooning

*A*s a psychotherapist, I often counsel couples who frequently argue. Early in my career I tried to help these people with communication techniques aimed at helping them be more open with each other. Yet, it rarely worked. They'd simply forget the method and continue with their verbal attacks. When I realized couples behave like hurt infants when they get into a fight, I asked myself, "What helps crying infants to feel better?" The answer was obvious—they like to be held. As parents gently hold their baby, the baby soon feels better. Before you know it, the infant is giggling and happy. I wondered if a similar approach might work with adults. After much trial and error, I found something that works even better than I expected. I call it "The Spoon Tune."

One of the great things about the Spoon Tune is how easy it is. When we're upset, we don't have the capacity to do anything complicated. Luckily, the Spoon Tune has just two simple steps to it. First, at the earliest sign of upset, lie down with your partner in "spooning" position. Spooning is the way in which many couples sleep. It consists of having one person's front side hugging the other person's back side. Couples can also "spoon" standing up if they're in a place where they can't lie down, or there's no place to do so. Although holding your partner in this manner is hard to do when you're upset, direct yourself to do it. Sometimes I think to myself that I have a choice between spooning for four minutes and feeling fine, or staying upset and ruining the rest of the day. When I clearly see that those are my two options, I begin spooning.

Next, while in spooning position, breathe in unison with your mate. Generally, it's best for the bigger partner to follow the breath of the smaller partner. When the smaller person inhales, the other partner should inhale. When the smaller partner exhales, the other should exhale. Hold each other and breathe in unison like this for at least four minutes. Don't say *anything*. As soon as your mind wanders, focus once again on breathing in unison with your partner.

No matter how upset you are at the beginning of this simple exercise, you will find yourself quickly calming down. The combination of being in the spooning position and breathing together puts people back on the same wavelength. When you share energy in this way, it creates a feeling of safety and connection at a very deep level. Although your mind may be racing and storming, your bodies and souls can't help but connect. By the end of four or five minutes, you may not even remember what you were upset about. At the very least, you'll feel more connected and safe, and be much better able to work things out without hurting each other.

One of the first times I used this method with Helena, my partner, I was extremely upset. After all, I knew I was totally right, and she was being totally unreasonable (isn't that always how it feels). Previously we had made an agreement that, if either partner asks for a spooning, we have to do it within five minutes. Yet, I was determined to keep being upset throughout the spooning—so I could then finish telling her how wrong she was. It didn't happen that way. Below is a transcript of the thoughts inside my head as I began to Spoon Tune:

"I can't believe she's making me do this. She is being such a jerk! She won't even listen to me because she knows I'm right." (We breathe together)

"I'm not going to simply let go of this. After this spooning is over, I'm really going to let her know how unfair she's being." (We breathe together)

"Well, I may have contributed a *bit* to the problem, but it's mostly her fault. After all, she's the one who started it." (We breathe together).

"Well, she probably didn't mean to hurt me. . ." (We breathe together).

"Perhaps I was also a bit insensitive." (We breathe together)

"It wasn't really that big a deal." (We breathe together)

"Gee, I sure enjoy holding her. (We breathe together)

"What we share together is really very special. I'm grateful this isn't a major problem." (We breathe together).

Four minutes are up. Helena asks me, "Was there something you wanted to say to me that you didn't get a chance to say?" I respond, "Umm, ahh, I don't really remember what we were upset about. I feel good again and that's all that matters." And that's really how it felt. Once the feeling of connection and safety is re-established through the Spoon Tune, there is no need or desire to argue. You feel like you and your partner are on the same team again. If there is still an issue to resolve, it's much easier to do so. Oftentimes, the "issue," which seemed so big just minutes before, has become totally unimportant.

Once you begin the Spoon Tune, *no* talking is allowed. If possible, find a place to lie down together. If that's not possible, "spoon" standing up. The key to doing this method successfully is to breathe together. As you breathe together, try to focus on and be present with each breath. Use your breath as a meditation. By focusing on your breath as it goes in and out in rhythm with your partner's breath, you will feel more peaceful, safe, and connected. Spoon for at least four or five minutes.

Once you're done spooning, you have a couple of options. You can simply forget about whatever led to the upset and go about your business, or, if you feel it's necessary, you can talk things over with your partner. If you need to work something out, you'll be in a much better frame of mind to do so.

You need not wait until you're upset to use the Spoon Tune. In fact, it's a *great* way to connect with your partner anytime. Many couples find it to be an easy and satisfying way to unwind after a stressful day. It can also be a very effective way to connect with your partner before making love. The hardest thing about this method is remembering to use it. Make an agreement that either you or your partner can ask for a "spooning" if you feel like your tempers are starting to get the best of you. Be on the look-out for times when you or your partner begin to get upset, or you both feel stressed. In order to use the Spoon Tune correctly the first time you get angry at each other, it's a good idea to try a practice run when you're not upset. Once you use it the first time and see how well it works, you'll be hooked.

2. How to Get People to Instantly Like You

Mastering the One Minute Relationship

Whether you're in sales, are looking for an intimate partner, or just want to make more friends, you need to learn to make a good initial impression with people. In the first minute of any encounter, we decide if we like and trust the person we're meeting, or if we would rather avoid them. Fortunately, there is a science to getting people to instantly like you. By learning how to create rapport with anyone you meet, you'll feel more confident and relaxed around people, and you'll experience more professional and personal success in life.

To master the one-minute relationship you first need to know what we each want—and don't want—from other people. Human beings all have a need to be accepted, respected, and appreciated. Conversely, what we fear is any form of rejection. When we meet someone for the first time, we subconsciously ask ourselves, "Is this person probably going to like me, or will they probably reject and/or bother me?" To answer that question, we look at various subtle clues in the first minute of our meeting, and from those clues we either feel connected or distant from the person we just met. In general, we tend to *like people who are like ourselves*. We feel safer, more comfortable, and more relaxed with people who walk and talk like us, and have interests similar to our own. Therefore, by becoming "similar" to the person you just met, there will be a strong tendency for that person to like you.

There are two ways you can use the "law of similarity" to build rapport with a person you just met. First, you can look for an interest you have in common, such as a person you both know or a hobby you both share. Have you ever been talking to a person, feeling like the conversation was going nowhere, and then they mention a topic you feel passionate about? What happened? Suddenly, there was a sense of connection. For example, if two people realize they each love ballroom dancing, they'll feel a bond with one another. Before you know it, as they talk about the intricacies of dance, they'll likely feel like old friends.

The problem with finding a common interest is that it's not always easy to do. If you simply ask someone about what they do for a living, it's likely you won't share the same line of work. Yet, there's a surefire way to immediately use the law of similarity with any person you've just met. By matching a person's *non-verbal behavior*, you become similar to him or her. To do this, simply notice how a person talks, sits, or stands, and attempt to "mirror" their behavior. Often, when we feel connected to a person, we unconsciously begin to mimic their body position. If, when you first meet someone, you talk at about the same speed as he or she, and hold your body in a like manner, you'll already have something in common.

On a subconscious level, the person you just met will feel a mysterious rapport with you. It works like magic.

Some people worry that if they sit or stand like the person they're with it will be noticed and seem weird. It won't. People aren't aware of their own body, so if you sit or stand like them, they won't notice it on the *conscious* level. But subconsciously, their brain will be saying, "This person is just like me—therefore I can trust them." By talking at about the same speed and loudness as the person you're with, you'll create another way in which you are alike. When people are different than we are, it makes us feel less trusting. On the other hand, when we immediately "hit it off" with someone, it's often due to the fact that they talk and stand in a way that's similar to us.

Many years ago, I had a dramatic experience of the connection that can come from this mirroring. Cheryl, my former girlfriend, had a father who was a military officer. At the time, I had a bohemian lifestyle living in spiritual communes, hitchhiking across the country, and so on. The information Cheryl's father had heard about me made him want to avoid me— because he viewed me as dissimilar to him. Yet, finally, Cheryl convinced her dad to meet me one time for dinner. He greeted me at the door with a frown on his face. His arms were tightly folded across his chest. He bellowed, "Well, Mr. Robinson, I've heard a lot about you!" I responded in a similar tone of voice, "Well Mr. Smith, I've heard a lot about you too, sir!" Cheryl thought I had suddenly gone psychotic. She had never seen me stand or talk that way.

Throughout dinner, I mirrored Mr. Smith. Although he wanted to hate me, subconsciously his brain was telling him, "This boy is just like you." Although he didn't know why, by the middle of the dinner, he felt a mysterious rapport with me. Soon, he became more at ease, and, as he did, I resumed being my normal, mellow self. After dinner, when Mr. Smith briefly left the room, Cheryl took me aside and said, "What did you *do* to my dad?" I said, "What do you mean?" She responded, "While you were in the bathroom, he told me he thought you were the finest young man he had ever met!" As this story shows, matching someone's body language and voice tone is an enormously powerful way to create feelings of trust and connection.

When mirroring someone, it's not necessary that you imitate every little movement they make. All you need to do is stand or sit in basically the same way as he or she. If he's sitting in a very relaxed manner, sit that way yourself. If he's standing straight and formally, follow his lead. Mirroring happens all the time without people being aware of it. The next time you're having a really good conversation with someone, notice how each of you is sitting or standing. You'll probably notice you're in roughly the same body position. By consciously matching the body position, voice tone and speed of people when you first meet them, you can *consistently* create feelings of acceptance and trust.

3. How to Overcome the Fear of Rejection

The Successful Rejection Experience

When I was seventeen, I was very shy—especially with attractive women my own age. By the time I was a freshman in college, I had only been on two dates. Driven by teen-age hormones, I really wanted to meet and go out with some women, but I was terrified of being rejected. My fear was like a prison, keeping me locked away in self-imposed loneliness. One day, I vowed I would overcome my fear. I decided that the only way I was going to become free of my fear was to plow my way through it. I enlisted the help of a good friend to make sure I had the motivation to face my fright head on. I gave my friend $50 and told him, "Don't give me this money back unless I get rejected by ten different women by the end of today." I figured that by experiencing ten rejections, I would know what it felt like and my fear would lessen. The money I gave to my friend would help me stay motivated to complete my mission.

I strolled down to the University Center to seek out attractive women. As I approached the first woman, sweat was literally dripping from my forehead. My knees began shaking, and as I said "Hello," my voice cracked. When the teen-age girl turned and saw me shaking and sweating, she worriedly asked, "Are you all right? Do you need me to call an ambulance?" She thought I was having an epileptic seizure. I assured her she didn't need to call an ambulance, and that I'd soon be okay. A brief, awkward conversation ensued before I finally mumbled, "Would you like to go out together sometime?" In a kind voice she responded that she had a boyfriend, but that she was flattered that I had asked. As we parted ways, I took out an index card from my pocket and marked down one rejection. Then, as I thought, "Only nine more to go," I began to breathe again.

Fortunately, each rejection got easier. In fact, I soon noticed that the women I spoke to seemed more nervous than I. My rejections were proceeding rapidly and smoothly until the seventh woman I approached. When I asked her for a date, she said, "Sure." I hadn't thought of the possibility of someone saying "Yes," so I said, "Sure what?" She finally convinced me she really wanted to go out with me. I wrote down her number, and in a state of happy amazement, soon asked another woman for a date. To my surprise, she also said "Yes." By this time, I was feeling totally at ease while I asked women out, and they frequently responded by giving me their phone number. In fact, after a while I had so many dates that I had to begin acting like a jerk in order to fill my quota of ten rejections (and get my $50 bucks back). After I had received eight phone numbers from various women, I managed to get my tenth rejection. In one magical hour I set up my love life for my freshman year *and* put a big dent in my fear of rejection.

From this experience I surmised that the key to overcoming one's fear of rejection is to set it up so that getting rejected is seen as a *success*. My actual *goal* was to get ten rejections, and only by doing so would I be rewarded by getting my money back. As I faced my fear, I saw that it wasn't so bad. I could survive. Since I was fully prepared for what would happen, it didn't seem like a big deal anymore. I noticed that with each and every rejection, it got easier. In addition, as my fear went away and I became more relaxed, I was often rewarded with an unexpected "yes."

Perhaps there is some area in your life in which the fear of rejection has kept you from moving forward. Maybe you've made success too important. Instead, try rewarding yourself for just making an *effort* and getting a "no." For example, you might decide to get three "no" responses to your sales calls each day, or one "no" per week from potential dates. My guess is that you'll survive. In fact, you'll probably get some unexpected "yes" responses along the way.

If doing an exercise like this strikes you as too difficult or scary, then you're probably a good candidate for it. To make it a bit easier for you, you can begin by asking someone to lunch who would not normally be your first choice for a date. After all, if they say "no," it won't matter to you so much. Once you've built up your "ability" to be okay in the face of rejection, you'll be better prepared to approach people who you really want to spend time with. Ultimately, the ability to face rejection is one of the most important skills a person can learn in order to create both personal and business success.

4. How to Start a Great Conversation with Anyone

The Instant Intimacy Question

*H*ave you ever been on a plane and wanted to start a conversation with the person next to you, but you didn't know what to say? Have you ever been attracted to a stranger at a party, but missed the opportunity to meet him or her because you were too afraid to introduce yourself? If you're like most people, situations like these happen fairly often.

When I noticed that I frequently failed to talk to people because I didn't know what to say, I set out to find a foolproof way to start a pleasant conversation with virtually anyone. To avoid looking ridiculous or desperate, I wanted to make sure the way I began the conversation did not make me look like a complete idiot. Commenting on the weather is one way to start a conversation, but it's so trite as to be embarrassing. After much trial and error, I came upon a method that can immediately lead to a meaningful, intimate conversation even with a total stranger. Mastering this method can transform your ability to meet and befriend anyone you desire, from a co-worker to a potential mate.

Before revealing the technique, it's useful to understand why it works. The reason meeting people is often difficult is because we're all secretly afraid of strangers. We fear that they might be weird, boring, or even reject us—which makes it difficult when you're trying to meet someone new. To help us overcome our natural fear of meeting someone new, it helps if we give people a logical reason why we're talking to them, and a simple way they can assist us. In addition, if you hope to have more than a brief conversation with someone you just met, it's important to ask him or her a question that can lead to a long, fascinating conversation. The Instant Intimacy Question accomplishes all these requirements.

The essence of the technique is to go up to a person you'd like to meet and say the following sentences in a sincere voice: "Excuse me, I'm wondering if you can help me out for a moment. I'm getting together with some friends later at my house to watch a video, and I want to rent a really great movie, but I don't know what to rent. I'm wondering if you might be able to suggest a movie that you thought was *really* good?" Once you say these three sentences, let the person you're speaking to think about it for a moment. If he or she has a hard time coming up with something, simply say, "Can you think of *any* movie that you liked that really touched you in a special way?"

Asking a person this question accomplishes several things. First, it begins some form of contact. If you don't talk to people, you can't get to know them. Second, it gives the two of you something relevant to talk about. Talking about the weather is a dead end, but talking about the movies each of you has enjoyed can go on forever. Third, the answer you receive will give you a lot of information about the person you just met. If he or she tells you they loved the movie *Friday the 13th*, then you know they might not be a good match for you if you dislike those types of movies. On the other hand, if he or she mentions a movie that you've seen and also loved, then you know you have some things in common. Lastly, when you ask people for their help and advice, it indicates that you value their opinion. Indirectly, you are giving them a complement, and most people enjoy being treated with such respect.

Once people offer one or two movie suggestions to you, you can naturally begin an enjoyable conversation with them. For example, if they mention a movie you've already seen, you can talk about how much you also liked that movie. You can even begin talking about what you liked about the movie, and why you thought it was so good. As each of you talks about your experience of enjoying a favorite movie, you'll notice that a feeling of connection inevitably takes place. If the person you're meeting recommends a movie you're unfamiliar with, then you can ask him or her what they liked about the movie. People like to talk about movies they love. It puts them at ease, and makes them remember a meaningful moment in their lives.

The Instant Intimacy Question can work in an amazing variety of settings, from parties to bus stops. This simple method can easily lead to intimate conversations *and* valuable information. After all, don't you like to know about good movies? Movies that become popular are like the shared myths and theatrical plays of olden days. They are powerful experiences shared by a large segment of our society. When you ask someone about a favorite movie, it immediately allows him or her to reminisce about an intimate experience. If you can share such an experience with someone you just met, it creates a powerful sense of connection in a short period of time. With a little practice you'll find the Instant Intimacy Question can easily create a wonderful connection with people you used to be too embarrassed to meet.

5. How to Easily Make Your Partner Feel Loved

The Love Strategies Concept

I have a question for you: for $500 could you make your partner feel upset in under one minute? Most people answer an emphatic "Yes!" To accomplish this, you would probably bring up some event, person, or question that invariably irritates your partner. We even have a term for this—"pushing my buttons." When someone pushes our buttons, it is commonly accepted we have no choice but to get upset. Over time, our partner usually learns where all our "buttons" are.

While "pushing my buttons" signifies a way our partner can easily make us upset, we have no phrase for the opposite effect—when our mate does something that invariably makes us feel loving. We could call it "pushing my love buttons," but there's no poetry in a phrase like that. I prefer to call it "charming my heart." When someone "charms" us, it's as if they have cast a spell of enchantment over our heart. A wonderful way to experience more love in your relationship is to learn of "automatic" ways to charm your partner's heart. When your partner feels fully loved by you, guess how they'll treat you? Soon, you'll both be charming each other's heart in an upward spiral that leads all the way to heaven. Ahhh, how sweet it can be!

In my book *Communication Miracles for Couples*, I talk about how it's necessary to realize each person has different rules or laws as to what true love is. Case in point: many years ago I was with a girlfriend I'll call Bonnie. I was giving her a nice shoulder massage when she suddenly blurted out, "Would you cut that out!" Totally caught off guard, I said "Cut what out?" She annoyingly stated, "You're always massaging me, you're always touching me, why do you have to be so grabby?" It was true—I frequently massaged her. So I said to her, "I do that to show you how much I care about you." She quickly responded, "Well, I don't *feel* very loved. After all, you never *tell* me you love me." She was right again; I never actually said the words "I love you" to her, although she frequently said such things to me.

Bonnie and I had a long discussion about this episode and we finally realized what had been going on. While I was growing up, whenever I was being spanked or punished, my parents would say, "We're doing this because we love you." Therefore, the words "I love you" had a negative connotation to me. I figured, talk is cheap. The way to *really* show a woman you love her is to touch her in pleasant ways. That was my "rule" of how real love should be expressed. On the other hand, while Bonnie was growing up, she had an uncle who frequently gave her massages. One day, this uncle sexually molested her. Therefore, she took my massages as being a precursor of impending doom. We both *thought* we were expressing love to each other, when in fact we were unconsciously pushing each other's buttons!

The way we tend to express love to another person is, in most cases, the way in which we would like to receive it. I gave Bonnie massages because that's what makes *me* feel loved. Even if a gorilla gave me a massage, I'd feel totally loved. Bonnie frequently told me she loved me because that's what *she* wanted to hear. When people are unaware of their partner's preferred ways of feeling loved, they end up expending a lot of energy that goes unappreciated. Yet by knowing exactly what helps your partner feel safe and loved, it becomes infinitely easier to create intimacy on a consistent basis.

There is a simple exercise you can do with your partner to find out how best to "charm his or her heart." Have him or her become comfortable in a chair, and then say the following: "Close your eyes, take a deep breath, and begin to think of a specific time you felt really loved by me. Remember that time as clearly as you can. Remember where we were, what we were doing, and exactly what happened that let you know I really loved you." Give your partner a minute or so to fully re-experience such a moment. Then proceed, "What was most important in letting you know I fully loved you? Was it something I said, or the way I looked at you, the way I touched you, or something else? *What exactly helped you to know that I really loved you?"* Listen carefully to what your partner says, because the answer(s) to this question can transform your relationship.

By knowing how your *own* heart is charmed, you can reveal this important information to your partner. Try the previous exercise on yourself, or have your partner read it to you. You may be surprised to discover exactly what your partner does that creates a warm feeling of safety and love in you. Once your mate knows how to help you feel loved, they can more easily and consistently show you they care.

Every time you charm your partner's heart, you're making a "loving deposit" in to your "shared love account." Your shared love account is like a bank balance you share together. When things are going well, there's a lot of love put into "savings." When both of you consistently make deposits into your shared account, you feel abundantly in love. It's *much* easier to handle problems when there's an abundance of love in your love account. Therefore, make frequent deposits of love in your relationship account by charming your partner's heart. Remember to do the little actions that make a big difference in how your partner feels. It will immediately help both of you feel wonderfully intimate, and when problems arise, you'll have plenty of love "banked" to help you ride out the storm.

6. How to Solve Problems with Anyone

The Amazing Problem Solving Question

Ron and Patty had only one big problem in their twenty-five year marriage. Unfortunately, because they never resolved how to handle the "chores" issue, they were constantly bickering. Despite twenty-five years of heated discussions, they hadn't made much progress. Like most couples with a thorny issue, they were still trying to decide *whose* problem it was, and the mere fact that they were still arguing about it made them even madder. At least once a week Ron and Patty would each present "evidence" to indicate that they were the one doing most of the work around the house. Secretly, they each hoped their partner would finally realize the errors of their ways, and apologize for their inconsiderate behavior. Of course, this never happened. Their attempts to show who had been doing more work around the house was a pointless waste of time.

Many couples fall into the same trap as Ron and Patty because they never actually *solve* any of their problems. As a result they have to keep dealing with the same old issues—as well as all the new ones that inevitably arise. Before they realize it, couples can feel buried by an avalanche of problems. The way to sidestep this trap is to learn how to solve problems—once and for all, no matter what the issue is. Couples who can master this skill find they can create a lot more love and a lot less conflict in their relationships. Of course, the importance of solving interpersonal problems is not restricted to the arena of intimate relationships. This skill can also make a world of difference at work, with friends, and when dealing with one's family.

To solve problems in your relationships with other people, first begin by stating your *positive reason* why you want to solve a specific issue. For example, in Ron and Patty's case, something like the following could be said: "Honey, I'd like to talk to you about the issue we have about chores. I don't want to make you wrong. I just want to work out something that would be agreeable to both of us. I'd really like to avoid arguments and instead spend more time feeling intimate with each other. Would you be willing to talk about it so we could finally resolve this issue?" When you tell people the ultimate positive reason *why* you want to solve a problem with them, they'll tend to be receptive to listening to you.

After presenting your positive reason for talking to someone, don't fall into the trap of presenting your "side" of the issue. Instead, begin by asking him or her The Amazing Problem Solving Question. The power of this question is that it gently directs people to think in ways that are helpful for solving the issue at hand. In addition, by asking the person you're dealing with to solve the problem, it prevents the two of you from bickering, and establishes your sincerity in looking for a solution. The question is, "*Considering my needs and desires with this issue, what do you propose might be a compromise that would work for both of us?*"

There are three possibilities of what someone will do when asked this question. First, they may present a solution that you find agreeable. If they do, tell them how great of an idea it is, write the solution down on paper, and keep your end of the bargain. If he or she says they don't have any ideas, or if their ideas are *not* acceptable to you, you can say, "Those are interesting suggestions you made. Would you be open to hearing some ideas I have that might work for both of us?" Since you let them go first, they'll feel obliged now to listen to your suggestions. When proposing possible solutions, try to present at least a couple of specific ideas. That way, they'll see that you're not dead set on a specific solution, and it will create a better atmosphere for compromise.

If you or the person you're talking with fall back into the blame game, ask the problem solving question again. Keep steering yourself back towards exploring solutions that are acceptable to both of you. You might ask him or her, "What is most important to you about (the issue at hand), or what most bothers you about (the problem)?" The more you understand each other, the more likely you'll be able to come up with agreements that truly work.

Sometimes it can be difficult to resolve an issue simply because people are afraid to agree to something that may not work long term. To avoid this problem, you can both agree to a specific solution for a "trial period" to see if it truly is acceptable. For example, in the case of Ron and Patty, they each agreed to do certain specific chores around the house each week. If one person failed to do a particular chore, they had to pay their partner $10 for each job that was undone. They agreed to try this approach for a month, and then discuss if they wanted to make any changes. At the end of the month, they both felt happy with how it was going, so they made the agreement permanent.

Recently, I had a problem with a printer who was always late in getting jobs done for me. Rather than blame him and make him wrong, I told him, "Joe, I value our relationship, and I want to continue to do business with you. I want to talk about something that's bothering me so we can clear it up and continue to work together. Is now a good time?" Joe was agreeable to talking. I briefly mentioned the issue of how my printing jobs weren't being done on time. Then I asked him, "Considering my needs in this situation, what do you propose might be a good compromise that might work better for both of us?" When Joe said he didn't know what he could do, I asked him if I could suggest a couple of ideas—and he agreed. Eventually, we negotiated that for every day my printing jobs were late, he'd deduct 10 percent off my bill. I was happy, and he was happy. Rather than end our relationship, in just a couple of minutes we worked things out to everyone's satisfaction.

What problems repeatedly arise in your intimate relationship—or your relationships with certain people at work? I encourage you to tell each of these people the positive reason why you'd like to solve this difficulty, and then proceed to the problem solving question. If you listen to their ideas with sensitivity and respect, they'll listen to you. Keep coming up with compromises until you find a solution you'd both be willing to try—at least for a week. Once you've tried something, you'll have more information about what worked, and if it didn't, how you might be able to change things so it will work the next time. The Amazing Problem Solving Question can be a lifesaver in your relationships with people, and it costs a lot less than seeing a marriage counselor, ending a friendship, or having to find a new job.

7. How to Quickly Feel Intimate with Anyone

The Spiritual Intimacy Experience

In my book *The Little Book of Big Questions* I have a chapter called "The Spiritual Intimacy Experience." It consists of fifteen questions that partners can ask each other to develop a deeper connection. I received many letters from people stating that answering these questions with their mate led to the most profound experience of intimacy they had ever had. In workshops I lead, I've seen that even when complete strangers openly share their responses to these questions with each other, a beautiful sense of bonding is created.

To enjoy the fruits of the "spiritual intimacy" experience, all you need is a willing partner, about forty-five minutes of time, and a somewhat quiet and private location. You can do this exercise with a lover, parent, child, friend, co-worker, or new acquaintance. Yet, since it leads to a deep level of sharing, make sure you do it with someone you'd like to be closer to. Below, you will find the instructions and the fifteen questions. Before you begin the process, make sure you have plenty of time, and are in the mood to fully open and connect with another human being.

Instructions:

You are about to begin an extended sharing experience. Really getting to know another person involves a learnable set of skills and attitudes, risk taking, trust, and acceptance. The following questions are designed to assist you in getting to know another person on a fairly intimate level. They can be answered to whatever degree of self-disclosure you wish. Take as long as you like to answer each question. Once you're done, ask the same question of your partner, and let him or her respond while you carefully listen. When you're the one asking the question, feel free to ask related questions that might further clarify or expand upon your partner's initial response. If a conversation naturally unfolds from your partner's response, that's perfectly all right as well. Once both of you have answered the first question, proceed to the next. If you give this exercise enough time and sincerity, I think you'll find it to be a very satisfying and powerful experience.

1. When are you the happiest?

2. What is your greatest strength?

3. What is your greatest weakness?

4. What was the most difficult time in your life?

5. What is extremely important to you?

6. When do you feel most affectionate?

7. What are you avoiding right now?

8. What helps you to feel really loved?

9. What is the thing you most regret having done?

10. How do you think I see you?

11. What is your heart longing for?

12. What do you consider to be your greatest accomplishment?

13. What was your first impression of me?

14. What do you like best about me?

15. What kind of person have you dreamed of becoming?

Besides being a great way to get to know someone at a deeper level, this exercise also demonstrates a process by which relationships can become more intimate. When we ask a friend or partner meaningful questions, it opens the door for a more profound level of connection with him or her. Most people hunger to talk about important topics such as the ones represented by these questions. Asking "big questions" is a simple and effective way to know the soul of another person—and experience your own essence as well. Yet, asking good questions is only half the story. The depth to which you can truly listen to your partner in a non-judgmental manner will determine the experience you have in this exercise. Try to listen with an open heart and a quiet mind.

If you enjoy this exercise, feel free to make-up your own questions. As long as you create an atmosphere of safety and warmth, people appreciate the opportunity to talk about themselves. In our fast paced world of gadgets and hype, the spiritual intimacy experience can be a great way to share the wonders of being human with someone you care about.

8. How to Immediately Deepen a Relationship

Your Last Call

*I*n his workshops on death and dying, author Steven Levine asks people a simple question: "If you knew you would die in exactly one hour, who would you call, and what would you say to them?" He then has people write down the name of the person they'd call, and the message they would want to convey. Mr. Levine then asks the workshop participants, "What are you waiting for?" Some people make elaborate excuses for why they can't make the call—while others simply go to the nearest phone and pour out their heart as if this were their last call.

When we become aware of our mortality, it puts us in touch with what's really important to us at our core. I've never heard anyone on their death bed confess, "I wish I had spent more time watching TV or at the office." In workshops I lead, I often guide people in a "ten minutes to death meditation." I have them imagine that they are going to die in ten minutes, and during this time I have them review their life. As people contemplate their life, I ask them if they have any regrets. I have them review the highlights of their life, and think about who they have loved, and who they will most miss. Then, I ask them to think of the person they will most miss and silently express what they would like to say to them before they "die." This simple little exercise leads most people to tears of sweet sadness, love, and gratitude.

When I saw how powerful an effect simply *thinking* about making a "last call" had, I knew I had to try it in real life. When I thought of who I would call and what I would want to say, my mind became filled with terror. I realized that this is a much easier exercise to *think about* than to actually do. Yet, I vowed to face my fear. Because I knew I might turn into a puddle of tears or immediately hang-up once I actually called this person, I decided to write down what I wanted to say. As I wrote my letter, I realized how much this person had meant in my life, and how I had never adequately thanked him. Tears of love and gratitude overwhelmed me. When I finally got the nerve to make the call, I began by reading the letter. Soon, I nakedly expressed my feelings without a "script." There were tears on both sides of the phone. It felt wonderful.

Making a Last Call, or writing a Last Letter is a remarkable way to deepen a relationship. It's a journey into the land of vulnerability and love. When we are conscious of death's calling, it helps us become aware of feelings that are normally hidden below the surface. Sharing your true, vulnerable and naked self with someone you love is a great gift for both you and the person you call. If calling and sharing from your heart seems too difficult for you to do, consider writing and mailing a letter that expresses your innermost feelings. By writing, you can feel assured that you will say exactly what you want to say. In addition, your friend or family member will then have a written reminder of a magical moment shared with you.

Besides deepening relationships, The Last Call can be a powerful therapeutic tool. A woman named Maggie recently came to my office distressed over the difficult relationship she had with her mother. Maggie and her mother had been locked in a power struggle for many years, and both felt frustrated and misunderstood. I suggested that Maggie write a Last

Letter to her mother so she could express different thoughts and feelings than she normally did. The effect of that letter was immense. Once Maggie had reached out to her mother in a new way, her mother responded in kind. Although they still have difficult moments in their relationship, Maggie told me her connection with her mother now feels totally different than before.

The Last Call idea need not end with one special person. It's a great way to deepen *any* relationship. People are hungry to hear heartfelt expressions of love, gratitude, and appreciation. The more you're willing to share your soul with people you care about, the more likely others will be to share their heart with you. Although you may find you resist this exercise because of its intensity, if you can get up the courage, I think you'll be amply rewarded. Why not give it a try?

9. How to Forgive People, and Not Judge Them

The Compassion Questions

Have you noticed that some people are just plain irritating? Either they're incompetent, or liars, or loud mouths, or bullies, or some people are even all of the above. If you don't live in a cave, you probably have to interact with such people from time to time. You may even have annoying people in your own family or house—which means you *really* have to deal with them. So how do you put up with people who "push your buttons," without becoming a raving maniac? Of course, you need to be able to set some boundaries with such people so they don't walk all over you. Yet even if you do that successfully, you're just doing damage control. However, by learning how to view "difficult" people with compassion, you'll feel better within yourself—and will likely help heal the troubled person you're dealing with. Fortunately, there are two questions that can almost instantly transform irritation into forgiveness, and judgment into understanding. I call them the Compassion Questions.

Before revealing the Compassion Questions, it's important to understand *why* some people are so annoying or hurtful. First of all, they often have very low self-esteem due to having experienced a traumatic upbringing. Because they didn't receive the love they needed as a child, they use destructive and desperate measures to gain recognition as an adult. Second, they are usually unaware of the effect of their behavior on other people. After all, what they really want is love, and their way of behaving certainly doesn't lead to that result. And thirdly, when they are judged by other people (even non-verbally), they feel lower self-esteem—and thereby become more annoying to be with.

Since when we judge people they feel more threatened, the best way to deal with difficult people is to avoid judging them in the first place. As they sense that you accept and understand them, they will tend to calm down and be easier to deal with. It sounds good in theory, but if you've ever had to deal with a truly annoying person, you know how hard it can be to forgive and forget. What's needed is a method that can instantly change your focus away from what annoys you, and instead allows you to focus on the emotional *pain* of the person you're dealing with. That's exactly what the first "compassion question" allows you to do. When someone is acting in a way you find bothersome, ask yourself, "*What pain must this person have experienced in the past in order to act so desperately now?*"

After you ask yourself this question, try to imagine the answer. Was the person you find annoying unloved as a baby? Was he or she mistreated by parents or teachers? Perhaps this person was criticized and rejected by everyone, and what you're seeing is the result of their pain. By imagining people as helpless, hurt little infants, you will likely feel some compassion for them. When you open your heart and let a little feeling of compassion in, it ends your annoyance. You can't feel compassionate understanding and irritation at the same time. By feeling or seeing the pain of the person you're dealing with, it will also help that person feel less threatened by you.

The second way to instantly forgive people and feel compassion for them is to see how their behavior is like something that you do. Often, we feel the *most* irritation at people who have an annoying behavior similar to one of our own—one that we try to hide from ourselves. For example, I used to get livid at a housemate who made a lot of noise in the kitchen. I thought he was incredibly inconsiderate of others. One day I confronted him about the clashing of pans and cupboards that he created. He shot back, "Well *look* who's talking. If your stereo isn't blaring, you're wailing on your guitar or singing off key." Indeed, he was right. Because I didn't want to think of myself as inconsiderate of others, I projected all my stuff onto him.

Once you're aware of how you do something similar to the person you're annoyed with, there's a tendency to be more understanding and to forgive. Therefore, the second "compassion question" is, *"How is that person's behavior like something that I do?"* The more *specifically* you can pinpoint a behavior you do that is like the one that bothers you, the more understanding you are likely to be. In the New Testament, Jesus is quoted as saying, "Why do you look at the speck of sawdust in your brothers' eye and pay no attention to the plank in your own eye?" By looking at the "plank in your own eye," you will automatically be sympathetic to the plight of the person you had previously judged.

Some people worry that being understanding or compassionate towards difficult people means you allow them to walk all over you. It doesn't. It merely means you view their behavior from a more clear, bigger perspective. When you ask yourself either of the compassion questions, it helps you to better comprehend the situation at hand. From a clear mind and an open heart, it is much easier to see the appropriate actions to take with a troubled person. Instead of adding fuel to the fire, asking yourself these two questions will help to trigger a healing process.

Ultimately, we are all very much alike. We've all experienced being in a nasty mood, and most of us have even treated other people like dirt on occasion. When we're in such a state of mind, it is only through understanding and caring that we are pulled out. The Compassion Questions are powerful. They can instantly transform your judgments into forgiveness and acceptance. Yet, because they are so effective, you may notice that your mind resists them. After all, feeling judgmental and self-righteous is a very safe and easy thing to do. Instead of using the questions with people who make you livid, begin practicing this method with people who just mildly annoy you. Once you see it can work with people you slightly judge, feel free to use these questions with people who really push your buttons. As you get good at turning annoyance into compassion, you will be helping to heal the heart of both you and others.

10. How to Easily Enjoy Better Lovemaking
The Naked Truth Exercise

houting from the covers of magazines, books, and videos is the idea that sexual satisfaction can be had by exploring unusual positions and techniques. Variety is supposed to be the spice of life. Although trying new things can spice up your love life, I believe that the greatest way to improve your sexual satisfaction is with your mouth—and I'm not talking about oral sex. The problem most couples have in regard to sex is a lack of understanding of their partner's specific needs and desires. By communicating openly about such subjects, two people can vastly improve their sexual experience in a matter of a few minutes. The problem is, most couples find it too embarrassing to talk openly about this subject. Therefore, I invented a method to facilitate the process of communicating honestly about one's sexual preferences. I call it The Naked Truth Game.

In my video *Intimacy and Sexual Ecstasy* I had a couple demonstrate The Truth Game. When the video became a bestseller, I received a lot of letters from couples who said this simple exercise had a profound effect on their sex life. To play the Truth Game, find a comfortable spot to sit with your partner. If possible, play some soft music in the background, hold each other's hands for a couple of minutes in silence, and then have one partner read the following rules of the game out loud:

Instructions for the Truth Game:

The key to creating more pleasure and satisfaction in an intimate relationship is good communication. Therefore, in this game each person will take turns sharing what they enjoy—and what they don't particularly care for—in their physical relationship with their partner. The goal of this game is to communicate all the specific things you feel about sex that you might normally be too embarrassed to say to your partner. By doing this, you'll find that you'll be much more attentive to what truly pleases your lover, and your partner will be more aware of what is really important to you.

To begin the game, have either person say one specific thing they enjoy about their partner's physical or sexual behavior. When the first partner is done, the other partner can proceed to say a specific thing that they also enjoy. Next, have the person who began the exercise point out a precise behavior they don't particularly care for from their lover. Once he or she is done, the other partner can proceed to say something that *they* don't enjoy either. Continue to communicate in this manner until each person has said at least three things they enjoy and three behaviors they don't care for. End the game by saying something you appreciate about your partner, sexual or otherwise. To help you better understand this process, below is an example of Tom and Linda playing this game:

Tom: I really enjoy it when you take the initiative in bed by wearing something sexy and "coming on" to me.

Linda: I get very excited when you kiss and hug me a lot after you come home from work. It makes me feel like you really love me.

Tom: Sometimes when you kiss me in the morning before brushing your teeth, you have bad breath. I wouldn't mind sometimes being romantic in the morning, but I think you'd need to use one of those breath sprays or mints before we could become intimate.

Linda: Sometimes when you're touching my clitoris with your tongue or your finger, you put too much pressure on it, or go too quickly. I like it when you take your time, and touch around it or on it a lot more softly.

Tom: I really enjoy whenever you initiate oral sex. It feels fantastic.

Linda: I like it when we spend awhile cuddling and you take time stroking my hair before we begin kissing and taking our clothes off.

Tom: I have a hard time when I begin to touch you at night and you kind of roll over and don't say anything to me. My feelings get hurt. I guess I'd like for you to say something supportive, even if you don't feel like making love that night.

Linda: I don't know what to do when you want to have sex and I'm not in the mood. I sometimes feel pressured, and that doesn't feel good. I'd like to be able to tell you

I'm not in the mood without you taking it so personally.

Tom: I like how you are always willing to listen about my problems at work, and how you give me shoulder massages when I really need them.

Linda: I really appreciate that you buy me flowers or little things that show me that you care.

After ending with an appreciation for your partner, you can ask your lover to clarify anything that you didn't fully understand. In addition, you can try to solve any issues that arose if it feels like the right time to do so. In most cases, men and women have very distinct and different sexual needs and preferences. Therefore, in a spirit of compromise, it's important to try to satisfy your partner's *most* important desires. By playing The Truth Game, you will both be moving a major step forward towards a more aware, satisfying, and intimate love life.

11. How to Make Good Friends at Work

The Intimate Coffee Break

*K*aren stared at the lime-green words on her computer monitor. The letters wouldn't stop bouncing around. Like a movie that slips in and out of focus, the words became dancing images of blurred colors. Although young, fit, and pretty, Karen felt old, tired, and burned out. If it weren't for all the tension in her shoulders, she would have fallen into a sleepy puddle on top of her keyboard. And yet it was only 3:30 in the afternoon. She thought to herself, "What can I do to get through the rest of the day?"

The light bulb in Karen's brain flashed, her face brightened, and she intuitively knew exactly what she should do: trade massages with a friendly co-worker! Massage in the workplace is no longer reserved for just the wealthy, the weird, or the weary. In fact, individuals and corporations alike are finding it to be a practical and joyful way of increasing employee satisfaction and productivity. Many companies hire masseuses to demonstrate how to give a five-minute massage to a fully clothed co-worker. The ooohs and aahhs that follow such demonstrations indicate that this healing art has a very bright future indeed. When you receive a massage from a co-worker, your shoulders become relaxed, and your smile becomes big and wide. When you *give* a brief massage to a person at work, you open the door to a deeper level of cooperation and friendship.

Unfortunately, there are still many offices in which the joys of "clothed co-massage" are still unknown. But, like laughter, massage is very contagious. Once introduced into a workplace, it has been known to spread like joyful wildfire. That's because massage does much more than relax people and make them feel good. It also has beneficial effects in employee relations and the overall sense of community in a work environment. When people are given permission to touch each other in a non-sexual way, communication barriers are lessened. People get along more harmoniously, and therefore work better together.

In business terms, mini-massages provide an efficient alternative to coffee breaks. Two workers can trade relaxing, yet energizing massages within a mere seven minutes, and then be more productive and alert when returning to their work. Everyone benefits!

In order to successfully plant the mini-massage seed in your workplace, here are some helpful guidelines: First, try suggesting the idea to a co-worker friend. Ask for a three-minute shoulder and neck massage in exchange for one in return. Briefly explain why you'd like to try this, and how it can be a great substitute for the traditional coffee break. I suggest you first introduce the idea of trading massages with someone at work who already knows and trusts you. By doing this, you'll avoid creating the impression you're trying to "pick-up" on a co-worker. When explained properly, most people can't resist the idea of a shoulder massage. Once you've selected an appropriate person, be honest about your lack of expertise, and ask your friend to indicate what feels good—and what doesn't. As your partner sits in a low back chair, start by kneading your thumbs into their upper shoulder area. Ask your friend if they would like soft, medium, or deep pressure. Massage, like any skill, is best learned through practice and good feedback.

As co-workers see you and your friend enjoy the benefits of massage, they'll likely join in. That's what happened at a halfway house where I used to work. One day I asked my friend, Jay, if he would like to trade shoulder massages. Like a drowning man being thrown a life-preserver, he grabbed the opportunity. Jay and I each looked so relaxed after our "coffee" break that soon other staff members were asking us if we'd be interested in a "massage exchange." Within a month, trading brief massages became a common practice, and led to a deeper sense of trust, harmony, and connection amongst the staff. Most people are thrilled to discover something new that feels good, doesn't cost anything, and is actually good for them. There aren't many things in life that can stand up to those three formidable criteria. Before you know it, people in your workplace will be trading massages as often as they now trade entertaining stories.

Of course, trading massages need not be reserved just for work. You can share this wonderful form of intimacy with your mate or any of your friends. Because people often have "emotional stuff" about any sort of physical contact, it's important to make clear that this is not a form of sexual touch, but rather a way to help each other reduce stress. Scientists have discovered that people need a lot of touch in their life in order to keep their immune system strong, but many people only get touched when they're having sex. Sharing massages with friends, co-workers, or even family members can be a great way to feel more connected, reduce stress, and help each other live healthier, happier lives.

I WOULD
VERY MUCH
LIKE TO KNOW
AT LEAST A LITTLE
ABOUT
THE UNKNOWABLE.

Connecting with Spirit

We all desire to tap into a deeper experience of love and peace in our lives. Various religious traditions provide different "tools" for helping us foster a higher form of love and peace. For example, in Christianity, prayer and service are highly recommended, whereas in Buddhism, meditation is emphasized. In my book *The Experience of God: How 40 Well Known Seekers Encounter the Sacred* I asked forty spiritual "experts" how they connect to the "heaven within." In my interviews with people such as the Dalai Lama, Wayne Dyer, the late Mother Teresa, Marianne Williamson, and Ram Dass, I learned a fascinating assortment of methods for diving more deeply into Spirit. These spiritual experts taught me many techniques that were new to me—but surprisingly powerful. My hope is that, by sharing some of these methods with you in this section, you'll experience more sacred moments in your own life, and a deeper level of connection to your soul.

For many years I've had a spiritual teacher who has helped guide me. Many years ago, he suggested I try singing devotional songs to God. As a highly intellectual person, I always cringed when seeing people sing in a devotional manner. Yet, because I trusted his guidance,

I tried what my teacher suggested. The second time I practiced singing in this manner, I felt like a ton of grace landed on my head. I wept for over half an hour. Finally, between my tears of joy I muttered, "This technique has definite possibilities." From this experience, I realized that people don't always choose or pursue spiritual methods that are optimally effective for them. That's why it's so important to try a variety of techniques to grow spiritually, and see what works best for you.

I like to think we each have a "combination style lock" around our heart. Our mission, should we decide to accept it, is to try many different approaches to see what "opens" our heart. If we try just one or two things, it's unlikely we'll find the magical combination that works. Yet, if we try many different methods, it's quite likely we'll discover something that works really well. In addition, by exploring new ways into one's innermost being, it helps us to avoid spiritual "ruts." Even in the relationship we have with our Source or our soul, we can fall into comfortable routines that lead to a lessening of aliveness. By being willing to try out new spiritual ideas and methods, we can open ourselves up to a deeper spiritual experience.

The average American spends only a few minutes a day doing any form of spiritual practice, such as prayer or meditation. Therefore, the best methods are ones that can have a profound impact on a person—yet only take a few minutes to do. In order to experience a very deep level of peace, I used to drive 200 miles to a Redwood forest and meditate for several hours. Unfortunately, this manner of experiencing peace was highly inconvenient to my daily lifestyle. Now that I know ways to experience peace in five minutes or less, I frequently use these methods to bring more peace into my day-to-day activities. Even if you have a very busy life, I think you'll find the techniques that follow are practical enough that they can warmly nourish your soul in just a few minutes a day.

1. How to Quickly Quiet Your Mind

The Magical Tape

We all want to experience a deeper peace in our lives, but most of us have little time to practice spiritual disciplines. As a teacher of spiritual workshops, I've looked for quick ways to help people to quiet their minds. In general, traditional meditation techniques take a long time to really have a major impact on people. Therefore, I've experimented with many other approaches for helping people let go of their worries, and instead melt into the serenity of their heart and soul. Of the many different things I've tried, I've found one formula to be so simple and effective that I heartily recommend it to everyone. I call this method The Magical Tape.

In essence, the Magical Tape is simply a cassette of your favorite, most heart-oriented and meaningful songs—all on the same tape. By having a tape (or two) of all your favorite songs, you can easily have access to deep feelings of love and peace. Your personal favorite songs have the ability to move you into your heart, uplift your spirit, and help you feel a depth of peace. In my own case, I originally created two "magical tapes." On one tape are all my favorite instrumental songs. I use this tape whenever I don't want to have to engage my mind in listening to lyrics. It's amazing how, after hearing just one of these songs played on my Walkman™, I enter into a totally different mood. On my second tape, I have all my favorite heart-oriented songs that contain lyrics I particularly like. Often, I'll listen to one of these songs whenever I desire to feel peaceful inside, or as a way to get me in the mood for meditation.

A man named Frank came to see me complaining of marital difficulties. As he entered my office, it was clear that he was very tense. He told me that his wife was fed up with him because of how stressed he was from his job as an air traffic controller. When he went home each evening, he'd spend the first three hours in front of the tube—just trying to unwind from his job. By the time he started to feel a bit relaxed and sociable, his wife was ready to go to bed. After asking him some questions, I learned that he enjoyed classical music. I suggested he make a cassette tape of his favorite classical works, and listen to a couple of songs in his car before entering his house each evening. When he returned to my office the following week, he told me that his wife reported, "You've become a new man." Apparently, ten minutes of classical music helped Frank unwind much more effectively than three hours of TV. By the time he walked into his house each night, Frank was relaxed, refreshed, and emotionally available for his wife.

For many people, music is an easy and amazingly effective way to become centered. I have coached many of my clients to carefully choose the type of music to play before key events in their life. Before an important presentation, they might choose a favorite rock 'n roll song. Before a romantic night on the town with their mate, they may choose a favorite love song. Before a time of meditation or prayer, they may choose some New Age or quiet piano music. By knowing what mood you'd like to "get into," and choosing an appropriate piece of music to assist in that process, many people find they can successfully manage their moods much more effectively than ever before.

Of all the possessions I own, the tapes of my favorite music and my Walkman™ are my most treasured. By listening to these tapes, I have almost immediate access to any feeling I want—without any cost, and no known side effects! In making the tapes, I looked through all the tapes and CD's I own, and carefully selected the songs that have always had the most impact on me. Recently, I even created a couple of tapes of my favorite rock 'n roll songs. It was a fun process. Once I found a song that was a favorite, I had it duplicated onto "the magical tape." You can do this by going to Radio Shack and buying a specific cord to go from a CD player to a cassette deck, or from one cassette deck to another. Soon, you'll have one or more tapes filled with songs to help you experience whatever you desire.

Over the years, my two original tapes have blossomed into seven tapes—two rock 'n roll, three heart-oriented cassettes, and two of musical compositions that help me feel peaceful. At least one time each day, I take a break from my activities and turn on my Walkman™, tune into the music, and drop out of my mind's constant concerns. Whenever I meditate, I always listen to at least one song to help me get quiet inside. Try it—you'll love it! After your five to ten-minute vacation, your mind will be clearer and your soul more soothed. With hardly any effort at all, you'll find that you're more centered in your heart and better able to handle whatever life throws your way. The hour or so it takes to put your initial cassette tape together will be amply rewarded by countless hours of peace.

2. How to Listen to Your Intuition:

The Feeling Right Distinction

In workshops I teach on spirituality, the most frequent question I get is, "How can you tell the "voice" of true intuition or God from the voice of the ego mind?" (For the sake of simplicity, I will use the words "intuition," "Divine guidance," and "higher self" interchangeably). Over the years I've read many books about it and practiced many methods. Unfortunately, there is no foolproof way to definitely say that one thought is directly from God and another is not. However, through experience I've come to realize there is a process by which we can better discern true guidance from mental garbage. I call this process of discernment the "Feeling Right Distinction."

To hear Divine will, first you must decide if you are willing to hear whatever answer you may receive. If you have already made up your mind about what's best for you to do in a particular situation, then it makes it impossible to truly hear intuitive guidance. Yet, if you are willing to surrender your decision(s) to your Higher Power, then you're ready to receive intuitive guidance. Before asking for such guidance, I often ask myself, "Is there any answer I might receive that I wouldn't be willing to listen to?" If there is, then I don't bother asking until I am willing to hear *any* answer to the question I'm asking. I have made a "deal" with my higher self that just because I hear a particular answer doesn't mean I have to *act* on it. Knowing that I have this "safety valve" has helped me to be receptive to whatever my intuition says.

Once I have surrendered to the possibility of any answer to my question, I take time to quiet my mind. In my own case, I meditate to quiet my mind, or listen to some favorite music. Then, I ask a specific question that is about a current concern for me. Generally, my question takes the form of, "What do I need to know or do to serve my highest purpose in relationship to (briefly mention situation)?" Then I wait as receptively as possible. Whenever I notice my mind trying to "figure out" the answer, I take a deep breath and simply try to relax and let go. I know that intuition does not grow out of a rational thinking process.

I have taught hundreds of people how to listen to their intuition, and what I've learned is that people receive Divine guidance in different ways. Some people actually hear a "voice" that sounds somehow unlike their normal inner dialogue. Other people see images or symbols that indicate what they need to know. However, most people simply get a strong sense of what "feels right." Often, this feeling of what is right seems to spontaneously arise from nowhere, yet there is a strong sense of certainty about it. It's like an "Ah-hah" experience. It's almost as if you knew the answer all along, temporarily forgot it, and now you've rediscovered it.

Since people experience connecting with their intuition in different ways, it's helpful to remember how you've received intuitive information in the past. Think back to a specific time you felt like you received Divine guidance. What made you think that this was *true* guidance as opposed to simply random thoughts? Once you can identify how you were able to discern your intuition in the past, you will know exactly what to look for in the future. Besides the fact that true guidance usually has a strong feeling of "rightness" to it, many people report they also have a feeling of openness or relaxation in their bodies, and a sense of peacefulness in their mind. Like all skills, the more you practice, the more likely you'll notice subtle distinctions that differentiate guidance from normal thinking and feeling.

If you practice the above method and receive no answer—or one that is unclear, there are a couple of things you can do. First, you can ask that an answer become clear to you sometime during the next week. I've often had the experience of not getting an answer immediately, but spontaneously receiving the guidance I was looking for days later while walking my dog. When we are persistent in asking a question, the answer(s) eventually come. It may even come from an unexpected source, such as a friend's conversation or a TV show. However the guidance arrives, there will likely be a familiar feeling of "rightness" or certainty that you now know what to do.

The second thing you can do when guidance is slow in coming, or you're not sure if what you've received is best for you, is to seek more information. You can pursue additional information in a linear, rational way by simply asking yourself, "Is there any person or resource that might know information that is relevant to my situation?" Once the rational mind is satisfied it has collected all the information it can, it is often easier to tune into Divine guidance. Some people make the mistake of asking for intuitive information merely because they're too lazy or afraid to research the relevant facts about their current situation. For example, I had a client who kept asking his guidance if he should buy a certain house. He secretly wanted to buy the house, and his desire was interfering with his ability to listen to his intuition. I suggested he get the house inspected and appraised to see if it was a good deal. He initially resisted, but finally relented. The results from the inspection indicated that the house was on the verge of falling apart, and should be avoided at all costs. Sometimes, intuitive guidance is not the most efficient way to make a decision.

If, after trying the above ideas and methods you're still not sure if you're receiving true intuitive guidance, then use the idea I present in the next chapter—"The Cosmic Hot and Cold Game." In this method, you'll learn how to use your actions as a feedback loop for staying in alignment with Divine guidance.

3. How to Align With Your Higher Self

The Cosmic Hot and Cold Game

Once a person learns to listen to their intuition, they need to avoid the trap of simply waiting to be "told" what to do in life. While intuitive guidance can be a great tool for discerning what is best to do, it becomes even more powerful when it is used in combination with taking consistent action. In fact, intuition and action are meant to work together to help you pinpoint what your Higher Self is calling you to do. To show you how these two can work together, let me use an analogy. Remember the hot and cold game you used to play as a kid? Someone would hide an object, such as a pen, and you would try to find it. Whenever you got closer to where it was hidden, they'd say you're getting warmer. When you veered from its hiding place, they'd say you're getting colder. Eventually, you'd get "red hot" and would find the hidden object.

I believe God is really playing the hot and cold game with each of us. God—or the universe—is continually sending us both intuitive *and* external messages as to whether we're in alignment with our Higher Self. There are two ways such messages are communicated to us. The first way we can know if we're on the right path is by listening to our intuition. If, upon asking for internal guidance we sense that something *feels right or true*, that's a message that we're getting "warmer." On the other hand, when something doesn't feel right, or is somehow unclear, that means we're getting cooler. It's time to re-evaluate the direction in which we're going.

The second way we receive messages about how we're doing is by the *external* feedback we get. For example, if you share your feelings with your partner and they tell you how much they appreciate you, that's a good indication you're on the right path. On the other hand, if you talk with your mate and they get irritated and upset, that can be an indication there is something off course. Either there is something wrong in your relationship or something amiss with how you express yourself. By listening to the inner and outer messages the universe sends your way, you can soon learn to steer yourself to the treasure that awaits you—being in alignment with your Higher Self.

When I began my career, I used a different technique for trying to figure out what I should do. I thought that if I meditated enough, God would speak to me in a booming voice and tell me exactly what I was supposed to do. I call this the "Moses model" for aligning with the Divine. Many spiritually inclined people believe that God will one day speak to them in a distinct manner and say, "You need to go this way!" After all, that's what He did with Moses, so why not with you and me? Actually, God didn't do that with Moses. Moses had to stumble along for many years on his own before he received direct and clear guidance from Spirit. I believe that we have to do the same thing. Only after a long time of listening to the hot and cold feedback we get from the universe does it become fully clear what God wants us to do.

I would like to say I've learned my lessons and am now done with the universal hot and cold game. Such is not the case. When my second book came out, *The Little Book of Big Questions,* I intuitively felt that I didn't need to promote it. Then my linear mind kicked in and told me I had to promote it or no one would ever hear about it. Over several weeks I managed to call over 300 radio and newspapers about my book—hating every minute of it. To my amazement, not a single person responded. The universe was practically screaming at me, "You're now freezing." Realizing I was off course, I went to a friend for guidance. She suggested I read the book again and get in touch with how valuable it is. She also suggested I don't try to promote it, but instead ask my intuition if there is any fun way I might let others know about the book.

While in meditation, I got the idea that, on Christmas Day, families could use the questions in my book as a way to talk about spiritual topics and keep the spirit of Christmas alive.

I made a single call to CNN about this idea, and they loved it. They interviewed me for a full 15 minutes about the book. The interview went extremely well. Then, the producers at *Oprah* saw this interview and decided to base an entire show on the questions in my book. With a single well-placed call and idea, my book now soared onto the bestsellers' list. Working in cahoots with Spirit is a lot more fun and rewarding than trying to push through your own agenda.

As spiritual beings, we have a subtle balance to maintain. One part of our task is to take a lot of action, learning from the feedback we receive—as in the hot and cold game. The other part of our task is to take action inspired from a deeper place within ourselves. In the above example, I took a lot of action, but it wasn't in line with my intuition. Therefore, the results were not good. Finding the right balance of intuition and action is an ongoing process. Yet, there are signs indicating when you've veered too far towards either side.

A sign that you're living by the "Moses model"—meaning you're not taking enough action—is that nothing ever gets accomplished. Taking action and failing is better than never taking any action at all. We've all known people who have grandiose visions of what they'd like to create, but never seem to do anything but dream. It's a shame because their ideas may be great, but they lack the "strength" to manifest their dreams. People like this need to dive into learning by action, making a few wrong turns, and becoming wiser from their efforts.

On the other side of the fence are people who are always taking action, but who never listen to what their soul is saying. They get a lot done, and sometimes even rise to the top of their industry. Unfortunately, their feeling of dissatisfaction is evidence that they are off course. Taking action predicated only on the desire for personal profit is damaging to one's soul, one's relationship with other people, and even damaging to the planet. It is only when we strike the right balance of taking massive action, guided by God's will as best as we can discern, that we can accomplish our dreams and have a good time doing it. By listening to intuition *and* to the feedback received from taking massive action (the hot and cold game), over time we can know what we're here to do and align ourselves with our Higher Self. Although it can be a long journey to find that perfect alignment, when it happens, it's pure magic.

4. How to Pray Without Ceasing

The Thank You Technique

In the New Testament (Colossians 3:12), Paul instructs people that "...whatever you do, whether in word or deed, do it all...giving thanks to God the Father..." Hidden in these words is a truly remarkable way to feel closer to God during one's daily activities. To make use of this method, it is not necessary that you be a Christian, although it is helpful to have some belief or relationship with God. In my book *The Experience of God*, I asked each of the forty well-known spiritual leaders I interviewed about their favorite method of feeling closer to their Creator. While the range of responses was surprising, the answer I heard more than any other was that of focusing on feeling grateful to God throughout the day. As Ram Dass put it, "Gratitude opens your heart, and opening your heart is a wonderful and easy way for God to slip in."

In Western culture, we often think of prayer as *asking* God for something. Yet, in many spiritual traditions, prayer is primarily considered a way of thanking God for the blessings in one's life. Many years ago, I received an important lesson about "thankfulness prayer" from a Native American medicine man named Bear. As a condition of being interviewed about his life, Bear requested we meet at a location sacred to his tribe. Once there, he suggested that both of us begin by offering up a prayer to the Great Spirit. My simple prayer was that our time together be well spent, and that it would serve our becoming closer to God. Bear began his prayer in his native tongue, as I listened patiently. After ten minutes of listening to the sounds of his tribal language, I began getting impatient. After thirty minutes of listening to his prayer, I was secretly irritated. While I grew restless, Bear looked like he was soaring as high as the eagles that flew overhead. Finally, after fifty minutes, Bear finished speaking his words of prayer.

Trying to hide my sense of irritation, I began my interview by asking Bear, "What *did* you pray for?" Bear's calm reply was, "In my tribe, we don't pray *for* anything. We give thanks for all that the Great Spirit has given us. In my prayers, I simply thanked Spirit for everything I can see around me. I gave thanks to each and every tree I can see from here, each rock, each squirrel, the sun, the clouds, my legs, my arms, each bird that flew by, each breath I took, until I was finally in full alignment with the Great Spirit." It was clear to me that this man really *knew* how to pray.

From Bear's inspiration and the wisdom of many others I've interviewed, I began trying this new method of prayer. To make this form of prayer practical in my daily life, I began by simply saying, "Thank you God for (whatever is in my awareness)." Sometimes I would "prime the pump" by first thanking God for things that are *easy* for me to feel grateful for. For example, I might say, "Thank you for my health. Thank you for such a beautiful day. Thank you for Helena (my partner)." Then, once I truly felt a sense of gratitude in my heart, I would use "thank you" as a "mantra" for whatever I was currently aware of. For instance, if I was driving somewhere I might say, "Thank you for my car, thank you for my tape player, thank you for this beautiful music, thank you for this nicely paved road, thank you for the man that just cut me off, thank you for the anger that he stirred up in me, thank you for the opportunity to practice forgiveness."

The secret of this technique is to see *all* things as gifts given to us by God to enjoy or learn from. Normally, we take virtually everything for granted, and rarely stop to appreciate the wonderful things we are given. It can be eye opening to realize that even middle class folks of today live better than Kings lived just 100 years ago. Yet, without the "thank you technique," all the amenities of modern day life can go unappreciated. Once you have used this method for awhile, you can even use it to begin to value things that are unpleasant. In the example above, getting cut off by an aggressive driver was not my idea of a good time. Yet, if I'm doing my "thank you" mantra, I'm more likely to see how such an event can serve me. From a higher state of mind, I can see that this driver is helping me learn patience, compassion, and forgiveness—three things I'm not very good at. Fortunately, there are many drivers and people who are willing to help me learn this lesson! Thank you God for all that help.

Like any mantra or phrase that a person repeats, repeatedly saying "thank you" can build up a momentum of its own as you use it throughout the day. However, it's important that it not become a mechanical mental exercise. With each thank you that is thought, it's essential to feel a sense of appreciation in your heart for the gift you've been given. Besides helping a person tune into an ecstatic feeling of gratitude, this method can also help a person become more aware and present in the eternal now. Normally, we spend a lot of our time needlessly worrying about abstract problems. By giving thanks for what's right in front of us, our worries can disappear and be replaced with an expanded awareness of what is currently occurring.

Once you've used the thank you method for awhile, it's possible to experience an "advanced" form of this technique. Instead of thinking the words "thank you for...," you can simply notice whatever you're experiencing in the moment and *silently feel* your gratitude to God for this being in your life. To do this, it helps to be very focused in the present moment, and feel connected to your Source. Even just after a couple minutes of feeling the gratitude for each step you take and each breath you breathe, you may feel an inner ecstasy welling up from within. That feeling is God telling you that your prayer has been both received and answered.

5. How to Be Moved to Tears of Love

The Pure Love Meditation

When I speak to people at churches and temples I often ask, "How many of you in the audience think that some form of meditation is a good thing to do?" Almost all hands go up. Then I ask, "How many of you meditate on a regular basis?" Generally, about 2% of the hands go up. In researching why most spiritually oriented folks don't meditate, I found out that they claim it is either too difficult to do, or they don't have the time. With this information at hand, I set out to develop a form of meditation that could be done in five minutes or less, and yet would be so powerful that it could move many people to tears of love and gratitude. After a couple of years trying various combinations of methods, I developed something I call the Pure Love Meditation. In the workshops I lead, I found that over 50 percent of the people who do this form of meditation become teary eyed. For something so brief and easy to do, it has a lot of impact.

The Pure Love Meditation has three simple aspects to it that all work together to quiet your mind and open your heart. The first part is to get comfortable in a chair with a Walkman™ or portable CD player, and play a song that moves you emotionally. It can be either a peaceful instrumental song, or a song that helps you feel loving inside. If you've created your Magical Tape (from Chapter One in this section), you can use a selection from that tape. Once a favorite song is playing, take a very deep breath, hold your breath for about five seconds, and then exhale with a long, slow sighing sound. Repeat this process three or four more times as the song plays, each time ending with a long sighing sound.

By now you should feel a bit softer and more relaxed inside. Now, it's time to focus on some person or animal you feel great love and affection for. It can be a child, a parent, a former lover, your current partner, your pet—virtually anyone. The important thing is that you have a strong heart connection with this being. Picture this person or animal clearly in your mind, and imagine him or her giving you a look that melts your heart. Think about the things you most love and appreciate about this person or animal. You can even imagine giving a warm, heartfelt hug to the one you love. With each breath, let your heart be filled with the love and affection you feel. Imagine your two souls being connected by the caring you have for each other. Once the song or songs end, continue to feel the glow in your heart.

Many people have found they can deepen their feeling of connection by thinking the words, "I love you," as they picture the one they are sending love to. Personally, I have found that when I picture my partner and call her by one of the many "endearing" nicknames I have for her, this helps me to feel my love for her even more. I recently discovered that if I imagine hearing *her* call me by one of the "pet names" she has for me, that also helps to melt my heart.

Although most people find they can go deeper into this experience if they do it while listening to some favorite music, some people prefer to do it in silence. You might try it both ways and see which one you enjoy more. In addition, you can use this same technique for just thirty seconds or a minute by simply doing a single deep breath and *then* thinking of the one you love. It can be surprising to discover that diving into an experience of love for just a brief moment can dramatically change how you feel. Studies done at the Institute of HeartMath have shown that focussing on feelings of love and appreciation for even a single minute result in a significant reduction in stress hormones for several hours.

The Pure Love Meditation is not only a way to feel love, but also a way to tap into the reservoir of peace within. Normally, during our day we get caught up in worries and concerns, and lose sight of the "bigger picture." By focussing on love, all the thoughts and worries that come from your head begin to dissipate. When your energy is centered in your heart, you'll feel quieter inside. In addition, doing the Pure Love Meditation can be an excellent way to help you get in touch with your intuitive guidance. As the mind quiets down and the heart opens, it's easier to distinguish true guidance from ego based thoughts. As you practice this meditation, you'll find it becomes increasingly easy to tune into the love and peace that's always inside you. The Pure Love Meditation is a practical way to build a bridge to the "kingdom of heaven within."

6. How to Know Your Mission in Life

The Near Death Questions

Back in the mid 1970's, Dr. Raymond Moody wrote a book titled *Life After Life* in which people described their experience of temporarily "dying" and then being brought back to life. Perhaps the most striking element of the book was the fact that people reported extremely similar events upon being pronounced dead. Almost all people who had a near death experience (NDE) noted they heard certain sounds, went through a tunnel, and eventually encountered a bright light that seemed to emanate love. Upon further investigation, various researchers discovered that most people who have had this experience felt they were asked two questions during the time of their "death." No matter what culture a person was from, or what religious beliefs they held, the two questions were always pretty much the same. I think of these two questions as the "final exam" of our life. They represent what God or our Higher Self is ultimately concerned about as we journey through our brief tenure on Earth.

In order to align ourselves with "God's mission" for us, it's helpful to know what these two questions are. The first question people report they are "asked" when having an NDE is, "*What did you learn about being able to love*?" It's probably no coincidence that almost every religious and spiritual tradition points to love as its core teaching and goal. In order to experience a deeper level and purity of love, there are many spiritual practices that have been passed down through the ages. For example, service to those in need, praying for others, and certain types of meditation can all be seen as methods to help us learn more about the experience of love. When we focus on feeling love for God and for all the people in our life, we become more aligned with our higher purpose.

The second question that arises for people who are near death is more complex than the first. Yet, there is still an amazing amount of agreement as to what is basically being asked. Roughly translated, the second question is, "*How well did you use your gifts to live your unique life purpose?"* Implied in this question is that we each have some specific contribution to make. Our mission, should we decide to accept it, is to figure out what our particular gifts are, and how we can use them to better the world.

Six years ago, before I had heard of the "near death questions," I had an NDE as a result of a car accident. Although I was being tossed around in a van that had overturned at high speeds, the two questions were my immediate companions. While close to death, I had the chance to review my life in relationship to the two questions. I was able to see where I had successfully aligned myself with "God's mission for me," and where I had not. When I was asked about how well I had served my unique purpose on Earth, I immediately understood that there were some books I was "supposed" to write that I had not yet written. Upon recovering from the accident, I soon began writing. In just four years, while maintaining a full time job, I've managed to write seven books and get them all published. People often ask me, "How have you been able to write so many books in so little time?" I tell them, "When you feel aligned with your Higher Self, you become filled with more energy than usual, and things can happen very quickly."

What are *your* unique talents and abilities? How can you use these gifts to contribute to the people around you and the world at large? How much have you learned about being able to love, and what still keeps you from being a more loving person? These are difficult questions to ponder. However, as you attempt to answer them, you can become more aligned with the underlying purpose and meaning of your life. In this age of countless distractions, it's more important than ever to keep track of the basic "tasks" our Creator has given to each of us. Only a life lived "on purpose," can feel truly meaningful, satisfying, and fulfilling.

A couple of years ago, I decided to ask myself the two "near death questions" on a regular basis. Now I take time about once a month to get quiet inside, ask the two questions, and then think about the answers. I ponder how effective I've been in learning about love and living my unique mission during the previous four weeks. By reviewing my life in this way, I gain valuable insights, and become inspired to stay even more aligned in the future. It helps me get back on track when I've veered from what is truly important—which is often. Yet, simply knowing I'm "accountable" to the near death questions on a regular basis has helped me stay on track more regularly. Try asking them to yourself right now, and then a month from now, and see if they can help *you* become more aligned to what's really important.

7. How to Make Major Life Decisions

The Vision Quest Experience

Have you ever been confronted with a major life decision and had no idea what to do? Perhaps it was a business decision, or whether or not to be in a relationship with a particular person. If you're like most people, you probably tried collecting all the information you could, but it didn't help much. In the end, you were forced to make an "intuitive decision." It can be scary to make a big decision without feeling assured you are making the right choice. For thousands of years, people from all over the world have faced this dilemma at some point in their life. Fortunately, there is a time-tested way that's been proven effective for making important and difficult decisions. It's called a "Vision Quest." A Vision Quest is basically a pilgrimage to a deep place within yourself that *knows* what's best for you to do. The rational mind is not particularly helpful in making many of our biggest decisions. After you've collected all the rational, linear information that's available, what's most needed is a method for contacting one's intuition (or if you prefer—one's Higher Self, Higher Power, etc.).

Rather than think of intuition as something that springs from nowhere, I think it's helpful to view it as something that's deep inside, waiting to be uncovered. Imagine a glass of water with a lot of dirt in it, and a clear diamond resting on the bottom. Because the water is dirty, the diamond can't be seen. Yet, once the dirt settles to the bottom of the glass, the diamond becomes obvious. In a similar way, once our rational, busy minds settle down and become quiet, the wisdom of our Higher Self can be easily ascertained. Yet, a Vision Quest involves more than just quieting one's mind. It also includes focussing on a particular issue or question with laser-like concentration. By combining a quiet mind with an intense focus on a specific issue, a Vision Quest can lead to important changes in one's life.

I stumbled upon the usefulness of a Vision Quest by having to face what seemed like an impossible decision. I had been in a relationship with a woman for almost three years, and we were in love. She wanted to get married and have kids, but I wasn't sure if that was the right thing for me to do. I knew that if I didn't soon ask her to marry me, she would want to break up. Confused and anxious, I decided to go to a favorite national park to get clear on what was best for me to do. I vowed I would stay and camp out at this place until I had received some "sign" regarding the right decision for me to make. As I drove several hours to the park, my mind became quieter. Throughout the day, I kept praying for clear guidance about whether or not to marry this woman. When I awoke the next morning, the answer was clear to me. Somehow, I *knew* it wouldn't be best for us to marry.

Although I felt like I had uncovered true intuitive guidance, after a period of time my rational mind kicked in and began doubting what I had received. Therefore, I asked for some sort of external sign to further indicate what I was being guided to do. Within an hour, a fellow camper walked up to me and began talking about how he wished he had never married his wife! That settled it. I now felt totally secure in knowing the proper course of action. The purpose of my Vision Quest had been accomplished. Although ending our relationship was difficult, it was made easier by the feeling that I had made the right decision. About a year later, I met a wonderful woman and we've now been a happy couple for over seven years.

I think there are four keys to receiving the answer you are looking for during a Vision Quest. First and foremost is the level of sincerity you have in asking for clarity. If you are committed to getting the guidance you seek, it will eventually make itself known to you. Second, to better receive an answer, you need to go through a process that quiets your mind. Depending on the person, this may involve hours of meditation or prayer, spending time in a favorite nature spot, or any other ritual that helps to calm the rational mind. Third, during the time of the Vision Quest, it helps to frequently ask for clear guidance as to what you need to know or do. And lastly, it helps to have faith in this process. People have relied on this method for thousands of years. You can relax and trust that, given enough time, the guidance you seek will become clear to you.

Occasionally, people receive guidance, but later come to doubt the answer they received. When I realized I wasn't to marry, I first felt completely at peace with this information, but I subsequently doubted it. Therefore, I asked for an external sign to "validate" my intuitive guidance. Although external signs can take longer to receive than simple intuitive guidance, they can be a valuable tool of last resort. Sometimes I have, in effect told God, "What I feel I'm being guided to do is (whatever message I received intuitively). If you want me to do *something else*, you need to indicate that to me with a clear sign by tomorrow, or I'll proceed with what I picked up intuitively." If no clear sign shows up by the next day, I feel assured that I made the right decision. By using the Vision Quest experience when faced with important choices, you can feel confident about making the best possible decision for positively effecting your life.

8. How to Really Enjoy the Holiday Season

The Best Christmas Present There Is

'T was the week before Christmas and in my own house I was frantic and hurrying, and felt like a louse. That was five years ago. That day I vowed I would never again get sucked into the hype of "Christmas Spirit." Instead of running around, fighting traffic, and losing my temper with store clerks, I decided I would do whatever it took to really enjoy the holidays. After all, it's *supposed* to be a time of celebration and spiritual renewal. Why not make it into one? Of course, if you're at all like I was, you're going to have to change how you "do Christmas" if you ever hope to truly enjoy yourself. I've found that four simple keys can help people turn their hurried holidays into heavenly Holy days.

First, try to remember the original purpose of the holiday season. Whether you celebrate Christmas or Hanukah, they both represent a time to appreciate the blessings of life, God's grace, and the end of darkness and the beginning of new light and hope. Can you remember a Christmas memory from your childhood that was filled with joy, comfort, and love? That's really what we all want to experience during the holidays. Yet, sometimes it seems we're being led down a fast flowing river that only leads to stress, insecurity, and even sadness. By having a clear picture of what a truly happy holiday season would be like, you have a fighting chance to create what you want. Without your own unique Christmas "fantasy" to hold onto, you're likely to be swept into the currents of what everybody around you is doing.

Once you have an idea of what you'd like to experience during the holidays, your next step is to figure out creative ways to avoid what you *don't* like about Christmas. For example, if you don't enjoy running around buying a lot of presents, then don't. Most people ask themselves the wrong question when it comes to planning their Christmas. Subconsciously, they think, "What *should* I do now that it's the holiday season?" If you "should" all over yourself, you'll never enjoy Christmas. Instead, it's better to ask yourself, "What would I *love* to do to spread joy and good cheer this time of year?" Listen for your own unique answer to that question. By following your heart, you'll feel the joy of Christmas, and enliven the spirits of those you love.

Each year when I ask, "What would I love to do this holiday season?" I get a different answer. One year I decided to simply write letters to friends and family and tell them how much I appreciated them. During another Christmas I sent people copies of favorite stories and jokes I had collected during the previous twelve months. No two Christmas seasons are the same. This year I've collected my favorite comics, copied them, and sent them to people I love. Although I rarely buy actual presents, many people have said they appreciate my gifts more than anything else they receive for Christmas. People like things that have a personal touch to them. How might you share with your family something that has brought you a smile or touched you in a special way? If you don't like to buy expensive presents, figure out alternative ways to express your love.

A third way to keep the spirit of the holidays alive is to give a present to your self. I don't mean another sweater or necktie. I mean something that will help you to experience the joy, peace, and sacredness of life. Last year, my partner and I spent three days in Yosemite in the middle of December. Leaving the craziness of city life for the grandeur of nature was the best present possible for both of us. This year we plan to go to a desert resort. As we sink into a jacuzzi bath while listening to Mozart, we'll be sure to reminisce about the madness we left behind back home. What would be some treat you could give to your self that would add meaning, joy, and relaxation to your winter season? Schedule it in now, before you get too swept up in the Christmas rush.

Lastly, to have a truly Merry Christmas or Happy Hanukah, plan ahead for something that you'd truly like to do. If you're not spending the Holidays with your family, call some friends and see if they're available. Perhaps you can create a meal together, play a fun board game such as Pictionary™ or Monopoly™, or simply have a meaningful conversation. In my book *The Little Book of Big Questions*, I offer readers over 200 questions that can spark lively conversations and help keep the spirit of Christmas alive. Perhaps around a Christmas dinner you can ask your friends and family questions such as:

1. What's your favorite Christmas (or Hanukah) memory?

2. What was one of the most special moments you experienced this past year?

3. What are you truly grateful for in your life right now?

4. What was the worst Christmas gift you ever received?

5. What gives you a real sense of joy in life?

Asking questions like these to those you love can help bring intimacy and a sense of the sacred back into the holiday season. Your fondest Christmas memories are probably not of presents you've been given, but of special times you've spent with people you cared about. Having a really good conversation with a friend or family member can be one of the best "gifts" you ever receive.

Although advertisements try to convince us otherwise, the holiday season is not a time of ease and joy for most of us. If you plan to have a good Christmas, you need to be *deliberate* about creating a sacred time with your self and/or the people you care about. By following your own heart, and keeping true to the original purpose of the Season, you can make this your best holiday season ever.

9. How to Easily Experience Your Soul

The Jaw Dropping Meditation

There's an old saying that "success leaves clues." This phrase basically means that if you do what successful people do you're likely to get similar results. I believe that people who experience higher levels of consciousness also leave clues. One manifestation of a higher level of being is the experience of "awe." When you imagine someone being in a state of awe, how do you picture him or her? Most people report they imagine a person with their jaw hanging open, and a completely relaxed look on their face. Recently, I had the thought, "If I totally relaxed my jaw and face, I wonder if that might trigger a spiritual experience?" To my pleasant surprise, it did!

The first thing I noticed as I tried to completely relax my jaw was that it was damn near impossible to do. People hold a lot of tension in their face without even realizing it. By attempting to completely let go of the tightness in one's jaw, it's easy to become aware of subtle tensions throughout one's face. In most forms of meditation, there is some precise thing to focus on—such as a mantra or a candle flame. In the jaw dropping meditation, the goal is to focus on the tension in your jaw and face. As you become aware of any tightness or holding, attempt to gently let it go. Eventually, you can reach a level of subtlety where you see that even each *thought* creates a slight tension in your face.

I have guided many people in this unique form of meditation, and people report different effects. Some folks report that it's a powerful way to relax their entire body and mind in just a few minutes, while others describe it can trigger profound "mystical states." On many occasions I've had the experience of letting go of my separate sense of self, and for a moment, merging with what felt like a "warm pool of loving energy." It can be quite exhilarating! When we let go of the "tension" of being a separate "ego," it's possible to merge with our spiritual essence, sometimes referred to as our soul or pure awareness.

In order to experience the jaw dropping meditation in a deep manner, I have found it helpful to be guided into it. Below I've written a paragraph to read to a friend as he or she does the meditation. Read the words slowly and gently, and whenever you see the word *pause*, take about one minute of quiet before proceeding to the next words. If *you* want to be guided in this meditation, simply speak these words into a tape recorder and play them back when you're ready for your journey within. As written below, the meditation takes about five to seven minutes. If you want to do it for a longer period of time, add your own words, or wait more than a minute after each *pause*.

Guided Meditation (Read very slowly)

Find a comfortable position, close your eyes, and take a slow, deep breath. On your exhalation, exhale with a long, slow sighing sound. Do this four times, and on the fourth exhale, let your jaw just drop open, and allow your entire face to completely relax. (Pause about one minute.) Focus on your jaw, and notice any subtle tension or holding. As you notice any holding, try to let it all go. It might be helpful to yawn if you notice it feels tight or if you can't tell if there is any tension. Once your jaw feels relaxed, you can focus on relaxing the rest of your face. (Pause). Once again, become aware of any tightness, and as you notice it, gently allow it to completely let go. As you let go of all the tension in your face and your being, you may notice you feel new sensations of being part of something else. You can't effort your way into your soul. You can only relax all resistance to being your soul. (Pause).

As you let go of all tension, effort, and thoughts, you will merge more fully with the present moment. When you completely relax your sense of self and become totally present, what remains is your pure awareness—your eternal soul. (Pause). If you want, you can slowly open your eyes, keeping your jaw, face, and entire body fully and completely relaxed. Imagine you just arrived into this body, and you are looking out your eyes for the first time. Behind the veils of who you think you are, there is pure awareness and love. Allow yourself to let go and merge with your spiritual essence. (Pause). Take as much time as you need to become aware of the room you're in. When you're ready, slowly stretch and move your body, stand up, and proceed with your day.

As with most forms of meditation, with practice you'll become better at it. Although it can be confronting to realize how much tension you hold, you'll soon find you're able to let it all go much more quickly than before. When you can completely relax your jaw and face, and open up to the present moment, you'll be left in an exquisite state of awe.

10. How to Feel Totally Peaceful

The Art of Mantra Meditation

Meditation has been around, in one form or another, for thousands of years. Yet, it wasn't until Maharishi Mahesh Yogi taught a simple form of meditation to the Beatles that it began catching on in the West. The Maharishi was the founder of Transcendental Meditation, better known as TM. For a somewhat pricey initiation fee, TM instructors taught hundreds of thousands of people a simple form of meditation that utilized a sacred sound known as a mantra. A "mantra" is simply a sound in Sanskrit that is believed to have a specific, soothing effect on the nervous system. By slowly repeating this sound to yourself, studies show that a very deep level of rest is achieved, and many people experience higher states of consciousness.

Herbert Benson, a research doctor at Harvard studied people who practiced the TM technique. He was very impressed by the changes meditators reported in their lives, as well as the physiological changes he measured in his lab. However, after studying people who did

TM for many years, Dr. Benson concluded that it didn't much matter what mantra a person used. He wrote that virtually any soothing sound, repeated in the way that the TM teachers instructed, would create a profound "relaxation response." Dr. Benson suggested that people use the word, "one" as a mantra, and save themselves the hefty price of the TM course.

Having been instructed in the TM technique, I agree with Dr. Benson that there is little advantage to getting your own "special" mantra. The main benefit to taking the TM course is the ongoing support it offers. In addition, when you spend a lot of money to learn to meditate, there's a tendency to stay with it—even when it's a bit difficult. On the other hand, when you read the basic technique from a book, you don't have the support and level of commitment of people who have paid good money. That being said, I'm going to reveal the basic technique here, and you can decide for yourself if you're committed to doing it on an ongoing basis. As with most spiritual growth disciplines, it gets easier with practice, and the benefits received are based on the time and effort you put forth.

In the TM technique or any form of mantra meditation, you first need to find a quiet time and place in which you won't be disturbed. Sit in a chair, with your spine comfortably straight, close your eyes, and take a couple of slow, deep breaths. After about thirty seconds, begin to slowly say the mantra to yourself (not out loud). For the time being, we'll assume you're using the word "one" as your mantra. Continue to repeat the mantra to yourself at a comfortable pace. *Whenever you realize you're thinking other thoughts, immediately (but gently) go back to slowly repeating the mantra: "one . . . one. . . one. . . . one."* Don't be concerned with coordinating the mantra with your breath—simply think the mantra at a pace that feels comfortable to you. After twenty minutes, or however long you've set aside to meditate, stop repeating the mantra, take a couple of deep breaths, and when you're ready—slowly open your eyes. That's it!

If you're like most people, you'll spend a lot of time thinking thoughts instead of repeating the mantra. That's okay. The one important rule to remember is that, as soon as you realize you're thinking something other than the word "one," immediately go back to focusing on the mantra. Your thought process might look like this:

"One…one…one…this is boring…oops…one…one…. I wonder how much time has gone by…one…one…one…one…one…I don't know if this is really doing any good. I should really be preparing for that meeting I have tomorrow. Oh no, I didn't even remember to get that woman's e-mail address. I need to…oh…one…one…one…one…one."

By going from mantra to thoughts, back to the mantra, you release stress and eventually enter a more refined level of consciousness. After twenty or so minutes, you'll likely feel very relaxed, much more at peace, and physically refreshed. It's twenty minutes well spent.

If you desire, you can choose your own mantra. It should either be one, two, or three syllables long, and have a soothing sound to it. For people who like to use two syllable mantras, I often suggest the words, "one love." Other common mantras include: Allah, Jehovah, Rama, Hahmsaw, and ohmmm. When you find a mantra that feels right to you, stay with it. Don't go changing your mantra for the sake of variety. Over time, you develop a "relationship" with the mantra you use in meditation, and you learn to "ride" it into ever deeper states of peace and joy.

To get the greatest benefits from meditation, it's important to meditate consistently. Maharishi Mahesh Yogi suggested people meditate for twenty minutes in the morning and twenty minutes in the evening. My personal belief is that any amount of meditation is better than none, and that being consistent is more important than how long you do it for. Although there are literally hundreds of different forms of meditation, I decided to include instruction based on the TM technique because it's so easy to do. The best form of meditation is the type that you'll actually consistently practice. If you know of a powerful method, but you never use it, then it's of little value. This form of mantra meditation has helped millions of people throughout the ages experience a deeper level of peace, harmony, and spiritual connection. If you make a commitment to practice it, it can have a major impact on the quality of your life.

I'M TOO BUSY
TO HAVE TIME FOR
ANYTHING
IMPORTANT.

Living Your Dreams

I believe that human beings are born with a dream inside of them—an idea or picture of how they'd like their life to be, and how they'd like to contribute to others. Whatever *your* inner calling may be, it needs to be nurtured. In this day and age, there are so many distractions that it's easy to get sidetracked from what you consider to be important. Like a fragile plant that needs the proper care to grow, your deepest desires need the right fertilizer and help in order to blossom. Of course, before you can live your dreams, you first need to know what they are. In this section, you'll learn tools to help you become clear about what's *really* important to you. You'll discover ways to keep your dreams vibrantly alive, despite all the distractions of modern day life. In addition, you'll learn methods to help you manifest those dreams efficiently, effectively, and consistently.

There are two reasons why it's important to be in touch with your dreams (or meaningful goals). First, studies show that people who are busy pursuing a purpose they find meaningful are much happier than those who feel they are not. Secondly, by manifesting your dreams, you become a stronger, more capable person. Ultimately, the type of person you *are* is more important than what you accomplish in the world. Yet, only by setting your sights on important goals can you develop the inner strength that allows your full *being* to manifest.

People are like lumps of coal. Hidden within a lump of coal is a beautiful diamond. Yet in order for the diamond to manifest, the coal has to be placed under tremendous pressure. When we face challenging tasks, whether it be becoming a parent or starting a business, we subject ourselves to pressure that can change us for the better. People like Nelson Mandela or the late Mother Teresa aren't born being great. They became diamonds through pursuing a purpose they found meaningful and important. As you pursue what *you* feel passionate about, you too can become the kind of person you've always dreamed to be.

I. How to Know What's Most Important To You

The Year to Live List

In order to be truly happy, people need to know what's most important to them. Only by focusing and staying true to one's deepest values can a person live an authentic, fulfilling life. When I proclaim such words in my seminars, I inevitably hear the question, "With so many competing priorities, how can I *know* what is most important to me?" Luckily, there is a simple way to ascertain what is truly meaningful to you. I call it "The Year Left to Live List."

When people find out they have a limited length of time to live, as if by magic their priorities become strikingly clear. I had a client named Sarah who found out that she had an inoperable brain tumor. Her doctors told her she had about four to five relatively healthy months to live, followed by a couple more months of increasing dementia. Sarah had been a hard-driving career woman who had worked about 60 hours a week. Her dream, or so she thought, was to become a partner in her law firm. Yet, once she found out her time was limited, she dramatically changed what she spent her time on. She immediately quit her job, took a trip to Israel for a month, and then spent her few remaining months surrounded by family and friends.

Unless you really *know* you only have a year to live, you're not going to be able to do what Sarah did. Nor is it what's called for. Yet, by writing down exactly what you *would* do with limited time, you can gain clarity regarding your true priorities. Once you're clear about what's important, you can more easily structure your time and your life in a way that leads to fulfillment. For example, if with a year to live you would want to travel around the world, spend time with your friends and family, and go on a whitewater river adventure, then these things are what really call to you. Although you may not be able to travel the world while holding a job, you can go on little trips and have mini-adventures. Only by doing at least some of the activities you'd do with a year to live will you feel truly satisfied with your life.

Most people make the mistake of continually putting off their dreams—hoping to get to them when they're all caught up. Unfortunately, new things are always being added to our to-do list, and our dreams get crowded out of our schedule. Usually, there *is* a way to spend time doing meaningful activities without having to drastically alter our life. Spending quality time with friends and family, taking little trips, spending more time in spiritual pursuits, etc. *can* be integrated into even the busiest of lifestyles. It's all a matter of prioritizing what you really value, and then scheduling these important activities into your weekly life.

You've read enough. Now is the time to make out your list. Get a piece of paper and write out at the top "What would I do with a year left to live?" Assume that you'd have the same amount of income you currently have, and that you wouldn't want to go into debt. Then, take only four minutes to write down all the things you would want to do. Feel free to abbreviate so you can write more quickly, but try to be as specific as possible. For example, instead of writing, "I'd travel," write out exactly where you'd like to travel to. Try to consider different areas of life, such as the following:

1. Who would you like to spend time with?

2. Where would you want to spend your time?

3. What adventures would you like to experience?

4. How would you be different in how you approached your life?

5. What, if any, legacy or contribution would you like to leave, and to whom.

6. What, if any, spiritual pursuit would you want to spend time with.

This exercise only takes four minutes, yet it can provide you with a treasure of valuable information. Once you have your list in front of you, ask yourself, "How many of these activities am I currently pursuing in my life on a regular basis?" If you're doing a lot of them, congratulations! That means you have managed to integrate what's important to you into your daily life. If its been weeks, months, or even years since you've done the bulk of the items on your list, then you need to work on creating the time for these activities into your busy life.

Perhaps you can take out your calendar right now and schedule a short trip you'd like to take, or call up an old friend you'd like to visit. It's critical that you do it *now*—before all the other competing priorities of life manage to drown out your dreams. Who knows—you may only *have* a year left to live. However long you have, this list will help make this next year a time of depth and quality.

2. How to Know Your True Work Passion

The Billion Dollar List

I magine you suddenly won or inherited a billion dollars. What would you do? You'd probably throw a big party, take the vacation you've always wanted to take, and buy a nice house. Then what? Although you may *think* you'd simply want to retire, most billion-aires continue to passionately pursue their work. Bill Gates and Donald Trump could easily retire, but they love what they do. In fact, studies show that the one thing rich people tend to have in common is that they greatly enjoy their work. When you love your career, you tend to be better at it, and are more likely to rise to the top of your field where the big bucks are. By imagining what you'd do with a billion dollars, it's possible to gain a better idea of what you truly feel is important work to be done.

Many years ago, I was taking a workshop in which the instructor asked everyone to write out what they'd do with a billion dollars. To my surprise, many people only thought of what they would want to buy. When the workshop leader read these responses, he added a new instruction: "Despite having a billion dollars, imagine that you were also *required* by law to work forty hours a week. What work would you do? In other words, what is work that you find *so* rewarding or important that you'd do it for free?" After thinking about what the instructor said, I decided I'd want to lead personal growth workshops, as well as write books that provide people with powerful techniques to improve all aspects of their lives. Now, a decade after writing down my answer in this workshop, that's exactly what I do for a living!

When you become clear about what you really love to do and what you consider to be important work, you become more focused and capable. Ten years ago, I was living in a 1967 Dodge van, making $400 a month. It seemed unlikely I would ever have a bestselling book and speak to millions of people a year. Yet, by consistently pursuing what I loved, it happened. Even if I didn't make much money or have much success in my field, I would *still* be enjoying what I do. I love teaching and writing. I'd definitely do it for free. Had I made the mistake of pursuing a different line of work just to make a lot of money, I'd probably be miserable. Many people make the error of putting their desire for money before their desire for meaningful work. Usually they end up paying a big price. Yet by figuring out what you'd do with a billion dollars, you can easily learn and start to pursue your true passions in life.

A billion dollars is one thousand million bucks. That's a lot of money. Would you want to help end starvation? Would you go into politics? Would you become a writer, inventor, or musician? What line of work seems like it's so fun or so important that you'd gladly do it for free? Take a few minutes now and write down a few answers to that question.

When I first looked over my billion dollar list, I became a bit depressed. After all, I wasn't doing any of the things I had written down. I had never done any writing, never been on TV, and was afraid of public speaking. Yet, I figured I'd start in small ways. I began by teaching a personal growth class to a few friends for free. I started writing things down just for my own benefit. As time passed, I got better at what I did. Before I knew it, people were paying for my workshops, publishers were buying my books, and TV producers were calling me to be on their shows. Since I really loved what I was doing, it was easy to be dedicated to it, even during times when I wasn't having much success.

Once you've written down what you'd do with a billion dollars, begin in small ways to incorporate some of those activities into your life. For example, if with a billion dollars you decided that you'd work to end the abuse of animals, then why not start to work in that area now? You don't need to quit your job to do that. You can begin by writing letters to your congressman, joining an animal rights group, or volunteering at an animal shelter. I know many people who started doing such things after they wrote out their billion dollar list, and later found themselves in a paying job working for the cause they had previously volunteered for.

The billion-dollar list helps you to think in a new, expanded manner. As you work in ways that are in line with your values and passion, you'll feel a sense of inner fulfillment. Many people report that initially making less money at a job is a small price to pay for work that is truly rewarding. Once you've made your list, you'll have a clearer sense of the direction you ultimately want to go in life. Then, you can use various tools from this and other books to help you more quickly manifest your dreams into reality.

3. How to Become a Genius in Life

The Joys of Journaling

The average person has approximately 50,000 thoughts a day. Of those thoughts, most of them are just like the ones you had the day before. Yet, occasionally you have a realization that is new, powerful, and potentially life changing. Perhaps it's an insight into how to make your relationship better, or maybe it's an ingenious idea for how to complete a project at work. Whatever your insight, it likely becomes lost as it's quickly overwhelmed by all the other thoughts in your head. Oh well. If you had only written it down, you could have reaped the rewards of your important realization. Yet, you don't have to let your bright ideas get lost anymore. By beginning a journal to keep track of your most meaningful thoughts, you can start cashing in on the genius within you.

In order to keep a journal that can have a profound impact on your life, you need to know how to properly use one. A journal should not be like a diary in which you simply summarize important life events. Instead, it should be a recording of your best ideas, deepest insights, and important dreams. A good journal becomes like a trusted friend, reminding you of where you want to go in life, and how you can best get there. By reading your journal periodically, you can trigger important new insights, as well as inspire yourself to take actions that can change your destiny. To make the most effective use of a journal, I have found six simple guidelines that can help you turn a book of blank pages into one of your most prized possessions.

To begin with, it's critical that you keep a journal near you at all times. You never know when brilliance will strike. For convenience sake, many people find it more beneficial to have a couple of small journals, rather than one large one. As an alternative, some people find it handy to keep a micro-cassette recorder or mini digital recorder around to record important thoughts. Then, when they have time, they simply transfer their taped thoughts into a computer file or journal. A recent addition to the art of journaling is to type your ideas into a laptop computer or personal digital assistant. Whatever your means of recording, it's important to have it near you at all times so that your important realizations don't get lost.

The best time to write in your journal (or whatever you're using) is the moment you think of something you don't want to forget. If you're in the shower or walking the dog when a great insight comes, immediately stop what you're doing and record your thoughts. I used to think I could write down my best ideas at a later time, but experience has shown me that I almost always forgot to do so. Because I get some of my best insights while driving my car or walking my dog, I now carry a micro cassette recorder around with me during these activities. Later, when it's convenient, I play the tape and record what I wrote in my journal. I have found that since my brain now realizes I take its insights seriously, over the years I've had many more important realizations than I used to have. Keeping a journal is like taking care of a beautiful flower. The more you attend to the brilliant "flowers" in your mind, the more they grow.

A third key to successfully keeping a journal is to structure it in a way that works most efficiently for you. Basically, people have to *discover* what works best for them. Some people derive the most benefit from their journal when it appears in outline form, while others prefer an unstructured way of writing. As you practice putting down your important thoughts, you'll soon discover what works best for you.

The fourth key to successful journal writing is to discern what to include, and what is best *not* to include. If you write too much in your journal, it will become boring to read. Yet, if you only use it for profound insights, it will not be as useful a tool as it could be. Once again, time and practice will indicate to you the most effective manner of making use of your journal. Personally, most of my journal entries fit under four categories or headings. These headings are: important insights, personal goals, actions I'd like to take, and creative ideas. You may want to come up with your own personalized list of categories that fit your unique needs.

Once you have gotten into the journal habit, you'll need to discover the best way of making use of its contents. I have found it helpful to set aside a small period of time each week to review the previous week's entries. In fact, the idea for this book came from reading the abundance of methods I had outlined in my journal. As you look over your journal entries, I think you'll be pleasantly surprised to realize the quality of your insights. True genius is not something reserved for a chosen few, but rather is something we *all* experience on occasion. By keeping a journal that records your most profound thoughts, you'll be able to make greater use of the genius within you. When you learn to consistently *act* on your best ideas and insights, the quality of your life will go through the roof.

4. How to Reach Your Goals

The Art of Manifestation

In 1953, a study began at Yale University in which all the graduating students were asked if they had written down their goals. Approximately 3 percent had written down at least one goal. For 20 years they studied how these 3 percent fared in life as compared to the 97 percent of Yale graduates who didn't write down any goals that year. In 1973, when they surveyed how these two groups did, they found that the people who'd written down goals were reportedly happier than the rest. They also displayed better health, a lower incidence of divorce, and greater career satisfaction. The researchers even learned that the 3 percent who had written down their goals were worth more financially than the other 97 percent *combined*. That means that, on average, they were making over 30 times the income of their classmates! Knowing what you want to create in your life, and writing it down as a goal, is a time-tested and powerful way to manifest your dreams.

Part of our journey as human beings is to learn to manifest our deepest desires on the material plane. In my workshops, I've guided thousands of people through the process of Dream Manifestation. I've seen what works and I've seen how people screw up. What follows is a brief description of five steps you can take to manifest whatever you desire. In this example I will use the goal of a man, Steve, with whom I recently worked with in my psychotherapy practice:

Step #1: Write down a single goal you'd like to achieve. If you don't know what you'd like to manifest, answer the question, "If I could create or have anything, what would it be?" When I asked Steve this question, he initially said he would like to have more money.

Step #2: Write down your criteria for recognizing when the goal has been adequately achieved. A criterion of success should be a specific and measurable description of exactly what you want, and a date by when you want it. Of course, it's important that your goal be realistic and attainable based on the effort you're willing to put forth. Steve decided he'd like to increase his income by 30 percent within one year.

Step #3: Brainstorm about the steps you could take that would help you move towards achieving what you want. Ask other people how they might go about achieving a similar goal. The more ideas you come up with, the better. You should be able to fill in this sentence: "Six or more things I could do to help me on the path of achieving my goal are . . ." In the case of making 30 percent more money, Steve's list of brainstorming ideas looked like this:

1. Work towards getting a promotion at work by finding out my boss's specific needs and doing everything I can to impress him.

2. Make helpful suggestions to my boss's boss.

3. Work extra hours so that the quality of my work improves.

4. Read a book on marketing so I can come up with ideas for selling more of our product.

5. Read a book on tapping into creativity so I can think of new ways to help the company.

6. Start writing articles that I can sell to a trade journal so I can make more money and become an expert in my field.

Step #4: From Step #3, create a logical order for doing the items you came up with on your brainstorm list. To do this, simply ask yourself, "Which item(s) would be best to do first, second, third, etc.?"

Step #5: Evaluate what's working and what isn't, and make appropriate adjustments. Keep breaking the big goal down into small steps. Do each task in the order you think will work the best for achieving the goal you desire.

That's all you need to do to manifest your dreams into the material world. It sounds easy, but there are many obstacles that can arise to make this process difficult. Some obstacles are unexpected events that life throws your way. For example, it would be harder to increase your income by 30 percent if your company downsized and laid you off. Yet, I've found that most of the obstacles that interfere with goal attainment are between our ears. You can't achieve a goal if you don't have one! Therefore, write a goal down *now*, and go through the five-step process I've outlined.

When Steve completed his goal sheet, he first tried to do too much at once, and ended up feeling stressed. I counseled him to take things one small step at a time. The next error he made was to ease off too much from the task at hand. For a couple of weeks he stopped making any progress. To overcome *this* problem, I had him write down the specific small action step(s) he would do each week in the direction of his ultimate goal. By slowly and consistently working on and completing the items on his brainstorm list, Steve soon saw he was making notable progress. Within nine months, he had achieved his goal—an increase of income of 30 percent. Steve was amazed at how fast his goal was achieved, as are many people who practice a deliberate plan for achieving their goals.

Whether your dream is of making more money, finding a loving relationship, or experiencing more peace, the process I've explained here can greatly accelerate your progress. The key to success is to have a plan, have a list of steps that move you in the direction of your goal, and have the patience and consistency to make small progress in the direction you desire. Why not take the first step in turning your dreams into reality right now? Create a "dream sheet" that details your answers to the five-step process I previously outlined. Put that piece of paper in a place where you'll see it everyday. Spend time each week working on the next step that will help you turn your dreams into reality. You'll be amazed at the results you can create.

5. How to Know What's Best to Do

The Art of Masterminding

We've all heard the adage "two heads are better than one," but when it comes to business and personal decisions, we rarely live by it. It used to be that a person could become an expert in many fields and have success as a "rugged individualist." However, that era has passed. Information in many fields is now doubling every two to three years. With change as rapid as this, to act effectively in life we need to be able to ask for and receive the help we need. People who are willing to get help from others are much less likely to make big mistakes in life, and much *more* likely to live their dreams. People who think they know it all or are unwilling to ask for help are increasingly being left in the dust.

I first learned of the value of receiving advice from other people in the first mastermind group I became part of. For those who don't know, a mastermind group consists of several people who get together to help each other in achieving their goals. Since I graduated high school and college with a straight "A" average, I had become a bit cocky thinking I always knew what was best. So, when four people approached me to be in a mastermind group, I figured I'd be a nice guy and help them out a bit. As we each took turns identifying problems in our business or personal life and asking for help, I got a bit snooty. The other members of the group had such simple problems to solve, and I was amazed at how they could have overlooked the solutions. I showered them with my words of wisdom, and they were very grateful.

Then it was my turn to ask for help. I didn't really think they could help me out because my problems were more complex, and besides, I was already doing *everything* possible to make things better. Wrong! The members of my mastermind group probably felt the same thing about me as I had felt about them. I think they thought I must have been a bit slow in the head to not know how to better handle the problems I presented. I was amazed at how much I learned from their counsel. As I implemented their advice, both my business and personal life got better. I had learned the value of being humble and receiving outside help.

To ask for advice from people doesn't mean you're not intelligent. It simply means you recognize your own limitations. A person who knows they need assistance and is willing to ask for it is at a great advantage in today's complex world. I often ask people questions such as, "What do you think is the best thing to do in this situation?" Two heads are indeed better than one. If you can get four or five heads together, all focusing on helping you, you'll be amazed at what valuable things you can learn.

The ideal number for a mastermind group is between four and six people. To start your own group, call your friends and ask them if they'd be interested in receiving free expert help in achieving their goals or handling problems. Explain to them it will only take a couple of hours, and that each person who participates will have a chance to receive business or personal advice from other members of the group. As well as receiving valuable feedback, they will also have the opportunity to help other people with the problems they present.

Once you've set up your first mastermind meeting, begin the group by stating that the purpose is to help each other, one person at a time. Decide how long each person will have to present their situation and receive assistance from the other participants. In general, thirty minutes is a good length of time for each person. Begin by having one member present what he or she would like help with. The more specific people can be in presenting how they'd like assistance, the more likely other members of the group will be able to supply useful advice. Once a person is done specifying their situation, the other participants can begin pouring out their suggestions. After approximately thirty minutes, the second mastermind member can begin his or her time for receiving help.

In the first mastermind group I was in, I wanted advice about marketing a video I had recently completed. I received many good ideas from people, but one particular idea was to try to get the video into various mail order catalogs. I hadn't thought of that before. Although I didn't think it would work, I followed up on the suggestion I received. I am very grateful I did because over the last seven years, I have made over $95,000 from that *one* idea! Mastermind groups can be very rewarding.

You can use mastermind groups for help with business, personal problems, marital advice—virtually anything. In just a couple of hours you can feel like you've received a wealth of good ideas, and also feel a sense of satisfaction from having helped other people. To insure the success of your group, choose people whose opinion you respect. In addition, make sure you give everyone in your group an equal amount of time, and have participants agree that all the information shared is strictly confidential. If you play by these simple rules, I think you'll find that your mastermind group will help you make more money, achieve your dreams, and will even lead to deeper friendships.

6. How to Quickly Become Just Like Your Hero

The Art of Transformational Acting

Do you have a "hero" or someone you wish you could be like? It's healthy to have people that inspire you to be your best. Whether you know your hero or not, or even if the one you revere died before you were born, it's possible to embody some of their traits into your own life. There are two primary ways to do so. First, you can work for many years to slowly develop whatever trait you admire in your idol. Characteristics ranging from courage to charisma can be gradually learned through effort and life experience. Yet, there is another possibility. Through a method I call Transformational Acting, (TA), you can become just like your hero *almost instantly.*

I first learned about the power of TA while at an expensive one-day workshop on acting. During the day, the instructor spent the first six hours going over a single technique. Basically, she took almost the whole day telling us that we needed to relax. After six hours of this incredibly boring repetition, I was about as relaxed as Charles Manson. I felt very upset about not getting my money's worth at this workshop. Then, she gave us the TA technique. The instructor told us to choose someone we admired who had a trait that was completely different from the way we currently felt. Since I felt like Charles Manson at the time, I thought I would try to feel the kindness and joy of St. Francis of Assisi.

The instructor told us to close our eyes and picture the person we admired. She guided us to "tune-into" the characteristic we most appreciated about this person, and to imagine we could literally "breathe in" this trait into our own body. From my upset state of mind I attempted to absorb St. Francis' energy of kindness and joy. Then, after a couple of minutes of tuning into a specific attribute of our idol, we were told to open our eyes and pretend to *be* that person. As we went around the room and interacted with other people, we were instructed to talk, stand, walk, and move just like our hero would do.

To my surprise, after only a couple of minutes of focusing on St. Francis, I actually *felt* kind and joyful. It was an amazing transformation considering whom I had felt like only a minute or two earlier. As I went around the room, I literally glowed with the joy of meeting amazing, new people. From my inner abundance, I showered each person I spoke to with love, acceptance, and joy. Soon, there was literally a line of people waiting to speak with "St. Francis," because they were hungry for the love and joy I was exuding. Internally, I felt like a completely different person. When I had "been" Charles Manson, my view of the teacher and the students was that they were all full of crap. Yet now, everyone seemed so beautiful—even the teacher!

Transformational Acting is a powerful way to quickly change how you feel. Yet, its deeper function is to help you grow towards becoming the person you yearn to be. By trying out new forms of behavior in this deliberate manner, you can immediately experience the joys and benefits of new ways of being. It can be reassuring to see that a specific attribute that you thought was a lifetime away could, in fact, be experienced right here, right now. In addition, I've noticed that "trying on" certain traits have helped me see what *interferes* with my growth. For example, by experiencing the joy and kindness of St. Francis, I could better see how my judgmental mind hinders me from being able to feel more love in my life.

Because the TA technique is so simple, it's easy to assume it can't possibly be as effective as it is. Only by trying it for yourself will you get to see how useful and potent it can be. The first step in using the TA method is to choose someone who possesses a trait you truly admire. It's okay if you've never met this person, as long as you have a clear sense of their positive qualities. Next, ask yourself, "What one or two traits does this person have that I would like to experience more of in my own life?" Once you know what you are aspiring to, visualize this person in your mind. Observe how they breathe, walk, talk, and interact with other people. Then, imagine that the one or two traits you selected are becoming infused into your own being as you take several deep breaths. When you feel ready, slowly open your eyes—while maintaining your connection to the qualities you desire.

The potential uses of the Transformational Acting technique are almost endless. If you need a boost of confidence before an important meeting, take a couple of minutes to tune into a favorite president or movie star. If you desire to be more loving, focus on emulating someone like the late Mother Teresa or the Dalai Lama. With practice, you can more quickly and easily learn to "merge" with a variety of traits "borrowed" from people you admire. In order to maintain the effectiveness of the TA technique, I recommend only using it for brief periods of time. By being deliberate about the situation in which you're using this method, you can keep your experience of it very crisp and alive. Before you know it, you may begin to *naturally* express many of the traits you previously had to "pretend" to have.

7. How to Get Your Life in Balance

The Daily Priority Challenge

Material poverty no longer exists for most Americans. Instead, its been replaced with a new form of poverty—a lack of *time*. Although studies show that we actually work fewer hours than we did thirty years ago, most people feel that they don't have enough time to do all the things they need to do. Why is that? Basically, we waste a lot of time doing activities that bring us little lasting value—such as watching TV—and forget to do things that add depth and meaning to our lives. In order to master your time and your life, every single day you need to prioritize what's truly important to you. Otherwise, you'll be swept into the river of distractions, and someday look back on your life and wonder where all the time went.

The problem with most time management systems is that they don't fully take into account all the different areas of life. Instead, they primarily focus on business. After reading about many methods of prioritization, I created my own system that was simple enough to use, yet powerful enough to create balance in my life. By sharing what has worked for me, I hope you'll incorporate some of my suggestions into your own life.

In my daily planner, I have a list of eight areas of life that I try to keep track of. They are: career, recreation, spirituality, level of fulfillment, bodily health, family and relationships, finances, and new learning. In modern day life, it's easy to get absorbed into just one or two aspects of life, and let the others fall by the wayside. Yet, to have a truly fulfilling life, it's necessary to create a healthy balance between all the competing priorities for our time. When we fail to create balance, we may look like we're successful in the short term, but in the long term we will either burn out or be unhappy. That's why I think about these eight categories of my life once a month. As I look at each area of my life, I ask myself, "How am I doing in this area? Am I spending the appropriate amount of time, energy, and attention on it?" Usually the answer is obvious. If a particular area of my life isn't doing so well, I vow to focus on it more during the upcoming month.

The next step in my system is to make sure I prioritize my day *before* I eat breakfast. I used to sometimes forget to set up my day, so I created a little reward system for myself. As soon as I'm done figuring out what's most important to do that day, I eat breakfast. Since I love eating breakfast (and never miss it), this simple way of rewarding myself for prioritizing guarantees that it always gets done. Then, as I look over all the things I could do during that day, I ask myself two questions. The first question is, *"What's really important to do today in order to create a balanced, happy life?"* This simple question gets my mind focused in the right direction. It's a much better question to contemplate than asking yourself, "What do I have to do today?" Asking about what's important helps remind me that the bottom line in life is not how much I do or make. Instead, it's how much of my dreams of creating joy, love, and contribution I can integrate into my day-to-day life.

Once I have briefly thought of the first question, I ask myself, *"What are the seven most important things I want to make sure I get done today?"* I write a brainstorm list of things I'd like to do, then I prioritize them from one to seven. Frequently, I include activities that are not business related, such as buying my partner flowers, or going on a bike ride. Over time, I've discovered that my career has its own way of getting my attention, so I don't have to focus on it as much as other areas of life. Whatever aspect of life *you* are most likely to ignore is the one that's most important to schedule. By scheduling your workouts, time with friends, or whatever you tend to overlook, your life will soon come into greater balance. If you don't get everything done on your list, write it on your next day's schedule. If you finish the top seven items before the day is over, ask yourself the two prioritization questions once again. It only takes a minute, yet its effect on your life will be immense.

By working with hundreds of clients in therapy, I've learned that people's lives are only as good as the worst thing in their life. For instance, if someone is rich, healthy, and beautiful, but their relationships are terrible, they'll feel rotten. It's a sad fact that the one area of our lives that doesn't work so well is the one domain that impacts us the most. That's why having a system that reminds you to work on your weak areas is so critical. As you create balance among the various aspects of your life, you'll feel happier and more peaceful. You'll spend less time distracting yourself from problems that could have been avoided in the first place. Rather than simply getting through each day, you'll experience the abundance that comes from feeling you're spending your time doing what's truly important.

8. How to Do Anything Difficult

The Proclamation Of Will Tool

When trying to commit to a major life change or decision, it's natural to get cold feet. Whether you're taking the plunge to have kids, buy a house, quit your job, or any other major life alteration, it can be useful to have a method that helps motivate you when the going gets tough. The Proclamation Of Will tool (POW) is a great way to keep you moving forward despite the challenges that inevitably arise on the road to your dreams. The POW tool helps a person in two distinct ways. First, it assists you in boldly and clearly deciding what you want to manifest in your life. Second, it helps to keep you motivated and acting in line with your dreams—despite the obstacles that inevitably arise.

In essence, the POW tool is simply a way to make sure you follow through with whatever important decisions you make in your life. For example, let's say you want to quit your job and start your own business. By telling your friends and family about your plans, it helps to make your decision more real. In fact, you'll soon find that the people in your life will *expect* you to follow through with what you told them. This can be a great motivator. No one likes to be seen as not keeping their word. To avoid the embarrassment of looking like a fool, people tend to follow through on whatever they proclaim to a lot of people.

The Proclamation of Will tool is really not anything new. Announcing an engagement to get married is a familiar example of the use of this method. Yet, this tool can be used for more than just marriages. In order to find a good use for this method in your own life, ask yourself, "*What would I like to do that I've been too afraid to commit to?*" When I asked myself this question many years ago, I realized I wanted to quit my job and take six months off to travel around the world. Before my dreams of travel became crowded out by my fearful thoughts, I began telling all my friends and family about my plans. Although I didn't yet have the money to travel, I had faith that if I proclaimed my dream enough times, I could eventually make it come true. One year after speaking my intention to all my friends, I managed to take a glorious trip through eleven countries. My trip around the world was probably the best six months of my life.

The POW tool basically has two simple steps. Step one is to decide what is something you'd like to do, and by when. It's best to choose something difficult, but important to you.

It might be losing twenty pounds, running a marathon, starting your own business, or any goal you know would normally be difficult for you to achieve. Step two is to announce to various people the exact goal and date by which you plan to "will" your dream into reality. The more specific you can be about your goal, the better. With each person you confide in, you help create a momentum of energy that is helpful in manifesting your desires.

In order to keep the POW tool powerful, it's best to use it only for important life decisions. In addition, it's critical that you consistently follow through on whatever you proclaim. Otherwise, you and your friends will eventually never believe anything you say. The power of your word is one of the most important keys for attaining personal and business success. When people see you can proclaim something and it actually gets done, their faith in you grows. More importantly, your faith in *yourself* increases. As your personal power grows, it becomes increasingly easier to manifest your goals.

I often get asked, "Who are the best people to declare your decisions to?" It depends on what your proclamation is. In general, it's best to tell people who will be supportive of whatever decision you have made. However, there are some decisions in which all the people in your life will need to be informed—even if they're not supportive. Getting married or traveling around the world are good examples of this. Of course, you can always inform people about your decision by writing them a letter, and thereby avoid an immediate unwanted confrontation. In situations where your proclamation may upset people close to you, writing a letter that explains your actions can be a good alternative.

Making life-changing decisions is a skill that can improve with practice. Most people avoid making powerful decisions or proclaiming what they want, and thereby miss out on a profound tool for manifesting their dreams. As you declare important decisions to your friends and family, you'll build up the power of your word. You'll find that you'll feel motivated to keep moving forward even when you face the obstacles and fears on your path. Like any muscle, the power of your word becomes stronger as you use it. Soon, you'll find that you can accomplish more with it. The true leaders of our day are the people who are known for committing to their visions. The Proclamation Of Will tool is an ideal exercise to train your personal power. The more you strengthen this ability, the more quickly you'll be able to manifest your dreams into material reality.

9. How to Be Motivated to Change Your Behavior

The Pleasure/Pain Description

Whether you want to end a bad habit, lose weight, make more money, or find inner peace, you need to master the art of motivating yourself. Although success in almost all areas of life is rooted in being able to *stay* motivated over a long period of time, most people don't have any idea how to do that. They simply *hope* that their enthusiasm will stay at elevated levels, despite the dampening effects of time and difficulty. Fortunately, you can now depend on a powerful method to help re-ignite your motivation whenever you desire. I call it the Pleasure/Pain Description (PPD). Using one of the basic principles of human psychology, the PPD allows you to quickly tap into images and ideas that will inspire you towards your goals.

The PPD is really a method loosely based on the Charles Dickens' story *A Christmas Carol*. If you remember, in that wonderful story three ghosts come to visit a mean, miserly man known as Scrooge. The first one to visit, the ghost of "Christmas past," graphically shows Scrooge how his behavior has hurt himself and others in years gone by. Then, the ghost of the present pays him a visit, and he also shows Scrooge how his lack of generosity has caused pain to those who depend on him. Finally, the ghost of the future comes by, and he shows Scrooge that if he doesn't change his behavior, he'll soon be dead and everybody will be celebrating. When Scrooge realizes how much pain he has caused himself and others, he finally decides to change. In a similar way, when you read your Pleasure/Pain Description, it will also help *you* to change—or stay motivated to do what you need to do.

The basic instructions for the PPD is to simply write out an accounting of exactly how your unwanted behavior has caused you pain in the past, the present, and if you continue—the future. Then, you write a brief description of how much *pleasure* you will potentially receive from staying motivated and completing what you deem to be important. The more specific and graphic you can make your description, the more effective it will be in motivating you. To help you get a better idea of exactly what such an essay would look like, I've included a *shortened* form of one below for someone trying to quit smoking:

"In the past, I've had dates not want to kiss me once they realized I was a smoker. I've had to endure the humiliation and the cold of smoking a cigarette outside in the rain, while everyone else had a good time inside. In the last twenty years, I've spent over $35,000 on cigarettes and increased medical costs due to smoking. If I had not spent that money, I could have owned my own home by now. Currently, I'm finding I get sick a lot more than I used to, and my husband doesn't enjoy kissing me anymore. Just trying to keep up with the kids makes me feel out of breath. I remember seeing how embarrassed Shelly was to introduce me to her friends because I had a cigarette in my mouth at the time. If I continue to smoke, I'm likely to die ten years earlier than I normally would (the national average). I can picture grandkids at my death-bed looking at me, tears rolling down their face, crying because their Grandma won't get to see them grow up. Yet by quitting cigarettes now I can save thousands of dollars, have more energy, have my entire family be super proud of me, and be able to romantically kiss my husband again. In addition, I'll be able to see my grandkids grow up and enjoy guiding them towards adulthood."

Although the above description is shorter than the one I would want you to write, it still creates some powerful images that can help inspire someone to stay motivated. The key is that you come up with pictures or memories that have maximal impact on you. By being clear about how your old behavior is causing you massive pain, and how a new course of action will bring you pleasure, you will automatically want to change. Among other things, I've used the PPD to help people off drugs, leave an abusive relationship, and even avoid eating sweets. Once you've written the whole thing out, you need only read it a few times a week to help keep you on track.

The most difficult thing about the PPD is taking the roughly twenty minutes to write out your list. Yet, once it's done, it only takes a couple of minutes to read it whenever you need to be motivated. An alternative to writing it out is to dictate your description into a tape recorder. As with a written description, the more specific and graphic your words are, the more motivating it will tend to be. Then, you can listen to it on your Walkman™ whenever you like. Once your PPD is done, feel free to add powerful new images as you think of them.

If you can dive into your mind and squarely face the consequences of *not changing*, you'll find, like Scrooge did, that you suddenly want to change. People are biologically programmed to avoid pain (physical or emotional), and try to gain pleasure. The PPD is a quick way to link pain to your old, unwanted behavior, and pleasure to a new way of being. Once your brain is clear about how it can avoid pain, you'll find that you're automatically motivated to do the right thing.

10. How to Stay Motivated Long Term

The Integrity Contract Method

What one trait would you say practically guarantees success in any field? Talent? Knowledge? In my opinion, the single most important trait for guaranteed success is the ability to be *consistent* in one's efforts. From Thomas Edison to Mahatma Gandhi, the most successful people in any field are those who can stay motivated over a long period of time. Unfortunately, people have a hard time maintaining high levels of motivation and effort. For most people, the inability to consistently act on their plans is what ultimately defeats them. Yet, there is now a method that is so simple and effective for overcoming this problem that, if you use it, your life will never be the same.

A basic rule of psychology is that people act to avoid *immediate* pain and/or gain *immediate* pleasure. I realized that, in order to have people make consistent progress towards their goals, they would need some form of immediate pain to occur if they failed to take appropriate action. Based on this principle, here's the essence of the technique: Write a contract with yourself that states all the precise actions you're willing to commit to do during the following week. Then write a statement that says, "For each of the items on this contract I fail to do by one week from today, I agree to rip up $2." The threat of ripping up $2 can be an incredibly powerful motivator. In fact, it can change your life.

I call this technique the I. C.A.N. method, which is an acronym for Integrity Contract And Nurturance method. The idea behind it is to increase the power of your word and nurture your dreams by consistently doing what's most important to you. There are several reasons why this method is so effective. First, there is a clear proclamation of what you intend to do, and by when you intend to do it. Normally, people have a lot of lofty *thoughts* about what they could do to improve their life, but these thoughts soon slip away. With the I CAN method, you'll have a visual reminder of what you're *committed* to do. Second, with this technique, you'll experience immediate pain if you fail to keep your word. Since your brain is always trying to avoid immediate pain, it will do its best to complete what's on the contract.

What follows is a step-by-step account of how you can use the I CAN method.

1. Sit in a quiet place and ask yourself, "What important things could I do this week to create a life of even more inner and outer riches?" Write down whatever ideas you get.

2. For the two, three, or four best ideas you come up with from #1, create simple, measurable tasks you can do within the course of a single week. For example, the inner message to "treat my customers better" might lead to the action of giving them a sincere compliment when you interact with them. To increase your level of inner peace, you could put on your contract one or two stress reduction methods that you think would help you feel more relaxed.

3. Write down on a single sheet of paper all the specific things you plan to do by the end of one week. Then, state that for each item you fail to complete by the end of the week, you will rip up $2. Sign and date your contract. Below is an example of how such a contract looks.

I, Jonathan, agree to do the following over the course of the next week:

a) Call five potential clients about my new seminar.

b) Wash my car, and put an ad in the paper to sell it.

c) Ask a friend to read my latest article and get her feedback.

d) Use the new method I learned to prioritize my day before I eat breakfast.

e) Meditate at least 30 minutes each day.

For each of the above items I fail to complete by 5:00 p.m. next Thursday, I agree to rip up $2.

(date)_____ (signature) _____

4. Put the contract in a place where you'll see it daily. Bathroom mirrors are good. So are car dashboards. If you have an appointment book, make sure you write down the exact time you plan to evaluate your contract. It's important that you schedule this. If possible, make this appointment exactly one week from the writing of the contract.

5. At the end of the week, evaluate how you did. If you didn't complete any items on your contract, no matter what your excuse, tear up the appropriate amount of money. It may take awhile to write contracts that work just right for you. Go through this process again for the upcoming week. Write a new contract that takes into account what worked for you in the previous week, and what did not. Feel free to write almost identical contracts week after week. After awhile, you'll find you can write highly beneficial contracts in a matter of two or three minutes. If you find you always miss items on your contract, write easier contracts. On the other hand,

if you find you always complete everything, put a couple of more difficult items on your list.

Think of how quickly you could turn your goals into a reality if you made progress on them each and every week. After awhile, the I CAN method becomes like a fun game you play with yourself. Rather than always putting off the dreams you have, it allows you to act on them right now. People who have the patience to slowly but surely make progress on their goals are the people who succeed in life.

From my experience of overseeing the I CAN process with thousands of people, I can say the single most effective way to ensure its success is to do it with a partner. When people try this process on their own, they frequently fail to rip up the appropriate amount of money. Yet, when you're accountable to someone else, it's a different story. Partners keep each other accountable and honest.

When I get together with my partner to go over the contract, he asks me, "How'd you do this week?" On a typical week I might say, "I missed one item, and I already ripped up the money." Then I ask him, "How about you?" After he gives me his answer, we hand (or fax) a copy of our new contract to each other. When we complete this process by phone, it literally takes two minutes. In the last three years, we've both increased our incomes and quality of life rather dramatically as we've practiced exercising the power of our word. If you can manage to make it through the first month, you'll likely become hooked because you'll be so pleased by the results you're getting. It's amazing, but true—the fear of ripping up $2 can keep you motivated to do all the things that you know would make your life better. When you consistently do the specific behaviors that make your life work, the quality of your life becomes incredible!

11. How to Stay On Track in Life

The Buddy System

*T*he great motivational speaker Tony Robbins often says "A lot of people know what to do, but few people do what they know." The Buddy System is a method that can help you take consistent *action* on what you already know will improve the quality of your life. This tool is given last in this book for a reason. The previous forty-nine methods, like any growth techniques, only work if you use them. The Buddy System is an unsurpassed way to make sure you consistently take actions that have a beneficial impact on your life. Whatever you want to create in your life, having someone who keeps you accountable to your important goals will help. A buddy can help you overcome the problems of laziness and distraction, and can be a critical ingredient that allows you to make your life a living masterpiece.

As I mentioned in the end of the last chapter, the Buddy System works great in conjunction with the I CAN method. There are many other advantages to using a Buddy System in your life. Besides the fact that it can greatly accelerate your progress towards achieving goals, it's also a great way to develop a friendship. In this chapter, I'll reveal what I've learned about using the Buddy System in a manner that's simple, effective, and maximally power-ful. After trying out some of these suggestions, feel free to adapt this technique to meet your own specific needs.

My buddy and I get together once a week. Like any appointment in our calendar, we choose a precise time and place to meet. When we're using the I CAN method, the first ques-tion we ask is, "How did you do on your contract?" As outlined in the previous chapter, if we missed any of our agreements, we rip up the appropriate amount of money. Then, we give each other a copy of our new contract. After going over our contract, (or if we're not doing a contract that week), we ask pointed questions about how each other is doing. What follows is a typical list of questions I ask my buddy in order to help him evaluate his life and goals.

1. In general, how do you think this week went?

2. What did you successfully complete this week that you're proud of?

3. What didn't you do this week that you would have liked to have done?

4. What do you consider to be important to accomplish during the upcoming week?

5. What would help you to stay on track towards doing what's most important to you during this next week?

6. What, if any, specific promises would you like to make for the coming week, and how did you do on your promise(s) last week (if you made one)?

As you ask your buddy these questions, listen carefully. You're free to ask any related questions that come up for you from the answers your partner provides. Your goal should be to assist your partner in discovering specific behaviors that interfere with progress, as well as to remind them of their important goals. Like a good coach, if your buddy needs a pep talk, give him or her an inspiring talk about the importance of realizing one's most cherished dreams. Once your buddy feels done answering the questions you posed, it's time for your partner to ask you the same questions. When answering the questions, really try to explore them in as much depth as possible. Hidden within those six questions is a wealth of information to help you get back on track in life.

Question number six is perhaps the most challenging question of the bunch. Although it is not required that you make a specific promise, it can greatly help accelerate your progress towards your goals. If you and your partner are using the I CAN method, then this question isn't necessary. Yet, if you're not, this question can help the two of you make precise promises without having to risk losing money if you fail to follow through. Your promise can be whatever would benefit your life, from vowing not to eat any cookies or ice cream, to declaring that you'll make more sales at work. By sharing specific and measurable tasks with your buddy, it raises the stakes of your partnership and, over time, increases the power of giving your word.

As you get to know your buddy better, you can begin to ask questions that are especially suited to meet each other's specific needs. For example, because I consider spiritual growth important in my life, my buddy always asks me how connected I felt to Spirit during the previous week. In order to answer that question precisely, I rate my week on a 1 to 10 scale. A '1' means that I never felt connected to the peace within, while a '10' signifies I spent most of the week in a state of bliss. You might try to use a similar rating scale to help you measure and evaluate important goals in your own life.

Depending upon the amount of time you have, you can have your weekly buddy session occur in person—or on the phone. The advantage of doing it on the phone is that the whole thing takes only about 15 minutes. The advantage of doing it in person is that it helps to deepen your relationship, and it can be a fun and inspiring way to spend time together. In my case, each week my buddy and I decide how and where our next meeting will be. If it's a busy time in our lives, we call each other. If not, we meet over lunch.

In seminars I often get asked, "Who is best to have as a buddy?" Typically, my answer is, "Anybody who is willing." I have seen the buddy system work well when it has been between husband and wife, roommates, parents and kids, co-workers, and even strangers randomly brought together at my workshop. To enlist a buddy, consider having someone you think might be interested in this process read this chapter. Explain to them that this could be a great way to help each other achieve important goals and make positive changes in your life. I think you'll find the buddy system to be amazingly effective in keeping you focused on what's truly important to you. Best of all, while you are helping yourself, you'll also be helping another human being to be all that *they* can be (without having to join the Army).

IF ONLY
I COULD GET
THAT WONDERFUL FEELING
OF ACCOMPLISHMENT

WITHOUT
HAVING TO
ACCOMPLISH
ANYTHING.

Ashleigh
Brilliant

Epilogue

*T*here's an old saying that if you buy a man a fish, you feed him for a day, but if you teach him to fish, you feed him for the rest of his life. Rather than temporarily "feed" you with ideas, I've tried to teach you practical tools you can use for the rest of your life. Over the years, the methods in this book have been like caring friends to me—always supporting me towards a life of greater love, success, and bliss. As I write this, I feel overcome by the feeling of gratitude for all the help I've received from these "power tools." I've seen that even using just one or two of the methods in this book can make a major difference in the quality of a person's life. I hope that someday soon you'll look back on the day you began reading this book as an important turning point in your life.

If you've read this book from cover to cover, you may be feeling overwhelmed by all the suggestions presented. My advice is that you take a moment now to choose just one or two methods from this book that you'd like to immediately begin using. If you haven't already done so, look over the Table of Contents *and decide on the method(s) you are committed to practicing this week.* Although the techniques in this book are among the best in existence, they don't work if you don't use them. However, in as little as two minutes of effort, these "shortcuts" can change how you feel, think, and act. Once you experience their effects, you'll be motivated to keep practicing them, and you'll be inspired to keep trying new ones. Perhaps you can put a Post-It™ note in an appropriate place to remind you about the method(s) you plan to use this week.

In the last two chapters in this book, I talked about the importance of having an accountability partner or buddy to keep you on track in life. It's important to have people in your life who will support you in becoming the type of person you want to be. I recommend that you tell your friends about this book so you can help *remind* each other of its many ideas and methods. By being accountable to someone for doing the small actions that make your life work better, you can get to the feeling of bliss even more quickly and easily.

In a world of increasing distractions from the joy and love we all yearn for, it's more important than ever to find shortcuts that help us stay true to our hearts. My deepest hope is that you'll use these tools to create more bliss for yourself, as well as more contribution to the people you love.

Acknowledgments

I want to thank the folks at Conari Press for their support of my work, and their commitment to putting out helpful and healing books. I especially want to thank Claudia Schaab and Mary Jane Ryan for their feedback and encouragement.

I did not invent most of the methods presented in this book. While the originator of many of these tools is hard to know for sure, there are some people I would like to thank for either inventing or popularizing certain ideas and methods:

To Tony Robbins for the "Love Strategies" concept, and the "Pleasure/Pain Description."

To Justin Gold for "The Compassion Questions," the "Jaw Dropping Meditation," and your unending commitment to helping me and so many other people.

To Jack Canfield for the "Mirror, Mirror on the Wall" technique.

To Napolean Hill for the "Art of Masterminding."

To Dr. Lou Stolis for the "Thank You" tool, and your inspiration.

And to Simon D'Arcy, Bruce Randall, and David Sampanis for the "Integrity Contract" method.

I am indebted to each of you for helping to bring such wonderful tools into the world.

I am also grateful for the friends that have helped me pursue not only the shortcuts to bliss, but also the long and often difficult path to awakening. In this regard I especially want to thank Amalthea, Arnie, and Edison for all your help.

Lastly, I'd like to thank my partner, Helena, my three parents and my brother and sister for their feedback, encouragement, and support.

About the Author

Jonathan Robinson is a professional speaker, psychotherapist, and author who lives in Santa Barbara, California. He specializes in providing people and businesses with practical tools for increasing their ability to communicate effectively, achieve important goals, and stay motivated long term. Jonathan teaches seminars and speaks to associations and corporations around the country. He has appeared on *Oprah*, CNN, and many other national TV shows, and his work has been featured in *USA Today*, and *Newsweek* magazines. He is the author of five other books, including the bestseller *The Little Book of Big Questions* and *Real Wealth: A Spiritual Approach to Money and Work*.

If you have a favorite method or idea you'd like to share for another book that reveals more *shortcuts to bliss*, please write, fax, or e-mail me (as indicated on the next page). Include your name, address, and phone number. If your suggestion is used, you'll receive credit for your idea, as well as several free copies of the book.

If you would like free information about Jonathan's talks or seminars, or a free catalog of his various books, audio and videocassettes, write to:

Jonathan Robinson
278 Via El Encantador
Santa Barbara, CA. 93111
Fax (805) 967-4128
e-mail: IamjonR@aol.com
http://members.aol.com/IamjonR/

Conari Press, established in 1987, publishes books on topics ranging from spirituality and women's history to sexuality and personal growth. Our main goal is to publish quality books that will make a difference in people's lives—both how we feel about ourselves and how we relate to one another.

Our readers are our most important resource, and we value your input, suggestions, and ideas. We'd love to hear from you— after all, we are publishing books for you!

For a complete catalog or to be added to our mailing list, please contact us at:

CONARI PRESS
2550 Ninth Street, Suite 101
Berkeley, California 94710
800-685-9595   Fax 510-649-7190
E-mail Conaripub@aol.com